SAINT MEINRAD
PRAYER BOOK

Saint Meinrad
Archabbey

---

*The quotations at the bottom of each page
are from the* Rule of St. Benedict.

Printed at Abbey Press
St. Meinrad, IN 47577

© 1995
ISBN: 0-87029-290-0
Printed in the U.S.A.
2nd Printing, 1996
3rd Printing, 2005
4th Printing, 2009
5th Printing, 2013

TABLE OF CONTENTS

Acknowledgements

Several people were instrumental in the original production of this book and should be acknowledged by name for their outstanding contributions.

Fr. William Munshower (O'58) and Mr. Charles Belch (O'64) initially proposed and subsequently shepherded this *Prayer Book* project. Their personal interest in the spiritual life, as well as their concern for the spiritual lives of others, is an example for many.

The original production of this book was made possible through the expertise of Ms. Barbara Crawford, who at the time was Director of Communications for Saint Meinrad, and her staff: Mrs. Jo Rita Bishop and Mr. Chris Blair. They wrote, typed and revised copy many times, and made sure all the incidentals of production were cared for.

In addition, Fr. Eric Lies, OSB, of Saint Meinrad was most generous with his suggestions and creative input. All of the calligraphy contained within this book is the work of his skilled hand. Besides adding the spirituality of those specific prayers, his artwork brings another touch of "Saint Meinrad" to the project.

Countless others contributed suggestions, material, "eyes" for proofing, and moral support in that original production of the *Saint Meinrad Prayer Book*. The help of each of those individuals was essential to the successful completion of this project.

In addition to the hands-on work of putting this book together, it could not have come to be without the generous support of the copyright holders of the information contained herein. These organizations and companies were most accommodating in allowing us reprint rights so that we could compile a publication that was spiritually useful and still reflected the "spirit of Saint Meinrad." The credit information provided below is listed in the order in which that material appears in the book.

• Permission for the reprint of the psalms has been granted by A.P. Watt Ltd. on behalf of The Grail, England. The psalms were taken from *The Psalms: An Inclusive Language Edition* published by the GIA, © 1993.

Preface

If there is one common bond among the alumni, monks, oblates and friends of Saint Meinrad, it is an appreciation of the spiritual life. For each of us, no matter what our current calling or position in life, an interest in things spiritual and holy forms the foundation upon which we exist.

That basis of spirituality stems from the environment at Saint Meinrad in which we grew as individuals—whether as a student, a novice or a guest. The Benedictine tradition of *ora et labora* became a thread that has been woven into our association with Saint Meinrad. Once you've been touched by that perspective of prayer and work, it is easy to see how one's spirituality, one's love of liturgy, and one's listening for God's call in life has been enhanced.

May Saint Meinrad's patroness, Our Lady of Einsiedeln, watch over all who use this book as a means of growing in the spiritual life and in the love of the Lord.

Introduction

During the 1992 Saint Meinrad Reunion, Fr. Bill Munshower suggested at the Alumni Board Open Forum that the Alumni Association publish a prayer book. Charlie Belch, a board member, promoted the idea at the next Board meeting. Then, in the spirit of Benedictine organization and tradition, both of us were appointed to serve on a committee to pursue the idea.

This prayer book is the most recent version of that idea, a project completed with much attention and excitement. We acknowledge the assistance of many staff members and alumni, who gave of their time and their ideas to help this book become a reality.

We hope that the prayers and even the appearance of this book bring you back to "the Hill." The Liturgy of the Hours is prominent. But the rosary and other private devotions reflect the spiritual life at Saint Meinrad. We have added some thoughts to ponder regarding reconciliation and end with a prayer for the faithful departed.

Our prayer for all users of this book is a union with one another, in God our Father, through our Divine Redeemer, Jesus Christ, and in the unity of the Holy Spirit.

Rev. William Munshower   *Charles H. Belch*

VENI CREATOR

VE-ni Cre-a-tor Spi-ri-tus, Mentes tu-o-rum vi-si- ta,

Imple su- perna gra- ti- a Quae tu cre- asti pecto-ra.

Qui paraclitus diceris,
Donum Dei altissimi,
Fons vivus, ignis, caritas,
Et spiritalis unctio.

Accende lumen sensibus,
Infunde amorem cordibus,
Infirma nostri corporis
Virtute firmans perpeti.

Hostem repellas longius,
Pacemque dones protinus:
Ductore sic te praevio
Vitemus omne noxium.

Tu septiformis munere,
Dextrae Dei tu digitus,
Tu rite promissum Patris,
Sermone ditans guttura.

Per te sciamus da Patrem,
Noscamus atque Filium,
Te utriusque Spiritum
Credamus omni tempore.

Gloria Patri Domino,
Natoque, qui a mortuis
Surrexit, ac Paraclito,
In saeculorum saecula. Amen.

VOCATION PRAYER

LORD, let me know clearly the work which you are calling me to do in life + And grant me every grace I need to answer your call with courage and love and lasting dedication to your will +

AMEN

The Life and Death of St. Meinrad, Martyr

Meinrad was born about 797 of noble Alemanic parents from southwestern Germany. The region of his birth was then known as Sülichgau, located between present-day Rottenberg and Tübingen. When he was old enough, his father brought him to the Benedictine abbey on the island of Reichenau, in Lake Constance, to be educated. His master was the distinguished monk Erlebald, a family relative.

Even as a lad, Meinrad was very focused, turning aside the childish behaviors of youth. The bright young student eagerly absorbed the teachings of his master and became quite knowledgeable of the Sacred Scripture. At the age of 25, Meinrad was ordained a deacon, and shortly thereafter became a priest.

After Erlebald became Abbot of Reichenau in 822, he encouraged Meinrad to consider the monastic life. Meinrad did profess the vows of monasticism and zealously strove to keep them.

After profession, Abbot Erlebald placed Meinrad as the head of a small monastic establishment at Benken, not far from the eastern shore of Lake Zurich, Switzerland. A school was attached to the establishment, and Meinrad passed on to the students the knowledge he had gained.

Yet even while he educated the youth, Meinrad felt called to a life of solitude, where he could enter into an

---

What, dear brothers, is more delightful than this voice of the Lord calling to us?

1

even more intimate relationship with God. His Abbot realized Meinrad's calling to be a hermit and, with the school closing, encouraged him to pursue this longing.

One day, Meinrad took a number of his pupils on a fishing trip along a mountain stream on the southern shore of Lake Zurich. While the boys fished, Meinrad explored the countryside along the ridge of Mount Etzel. He found himself drawn to the solitude. Inquiring, he discovered faithful in the nearby village who were willing to provide for his needs if he decided to retreat to the prayerful quiet of the countryside.

In 828, with the approval of his Abbot, Meinrad erected his hermitage on Mount Etzel, about two miles from Lake Zurich. He spent seven years there, devoting himself to prayer and to things of the spirit. However, word of his holiness spread, and gradually multitudes of people came to seek his counsel. Meinrad sought a more secluded spot.

Meinrad established a new hermitage—with the help of other hermits in the area—about a mile and a half further between the mountains, in an area known as the Dark Forest. His hermitage consisted of a chapel, dedicated to the Blessed Virgin, and a dwelling. He lived there for 26 years.

Periodically, Meinrad would receive gifts from charitable friends or from the faithful expressing gratitude for his spiritual help. But these gifts were usually given

---

The first step of humility, then, is that a man keeps the fear of God always before his eyes and never forgets it.

away as alms to those in need who visited him at his hermitage. Occasionally, his former confreres visited him at the *Einsiedelei* (hermitage), and several had reported celestial visits to the hermit Meinrad. One monk, in particular, told of a visit to Meinrad by a "child of wonderous beauty in white robes." The child, who seemed about seven years old, came from the oratory and went to speak with Meinrad. As he lay on his bed and watched, the child and Meinrad prayed together and discussed various things. While the visiting monk could hear the sound of the conversation, he couldn't understand it. Later, Meinrad would say that he was forbidden to talk about the visit.

One evening, two men inquired at the village about the hermitage. They were given directions and set off to find the hermit's cell. Believing that Meinrad possessed valuables because of his visitors, they decided that they would kill the monk, if necessary, to get the treasures.

The thieves arrived at the hermitage just as Meinrad was finishing Mass. Having received a premonition of his impending death, Meinrad prayed all the more fervently, recommending his soul to the Lord and the saints whose relics he held in his chapel. Watching him through a hole in the wall, the robbers surmised that the relics were treasures and demanded Meinrad open the door.

Meinrad did open the door and invited them to enter the chapel to pray as he prepared some refresh-

---

This message of mine is for you, then, if you are ready to give up your own will.

ments. The thieves, however, disappointed that the chapel held no visible treasures, followed Meinrad into his dwelling. Meinrad gave them some of his clothing and offered bread and drink. They demanded his valuables.

Because he knew of his impending death, Meinrad noted to the thieves that they could take whatever they wished after they had done their deed. He also asked that they place a lighted candle at his head and foot before they left.

The robbers then began to beat him with their fists and a club until he was half-dead, and then strangled him until he breathed his last. They stripped him of his clothes, placed him in his bed and covered him, and then placed an unlit candle near his head. After returning from the chapel with fire to light the second candle, they found that the first candle was already blazing brightly. Frightened, they grabbed a few items of clothing, ignored the sacred relics, and ran from the hermitage.

During his time at the hermitage, Meinrad often fed two ravens who visited there. As the murderers departed, the birds followed them back through the woods and into town, cawing excitedly and occasionally darting at their heads. When the villagers witnessed this display, they held the men until townspeople could determine the cause of such a commotion. They found the martyred Meinrad in his bed. The date was January 21, 861.

Listen readily to holy reading.

After court proceedings, the two murderers were burned alive as their punishment.

From the moment of his death, Meinrad was held to be a saint and martyr. The monks from Reichenau retrieved Meinrad's body from the hermitage and buried it at the monastery. On October 6, 1039, his main relics were reinterred at his hermitage; and about that time, Pope Benedict IX added Meinrad to the list of saints.

Clothed then with faith and the performance of good works, let us set out on this way.

Dilecte Martyr Numini

Dilecte Martyr Numini
Meinrade concinentium
Benignus aurem fervidis
Accomoda suspiriis,
Accomoda suspiriis.

Tu passus olim verbera
Diramque mortem; gloria
Nunc Laureatus, martyrum
Vestiris inter purpuras,
Vestiris inter purpuras.

Praeter fluentis saeculi
Quas vana mens praestigias
Exosculatur, praevio
Ductore Christo spreveras,
Ductore Christo spreveras.

Hinc luce solis clarior
Nitescis inter caelites,
Securus ejus praemii
Pro quo merendo caesus es,
pro quo merendo caesus es.

Ergo preced exaudias,
quas supplicas effundimus;
Causamque nostram sustine
Coram tremendo Judice,
Coram tremendo Judice.

Patri sit hymnus optimo,
Sit Filio laus maximo,
Suavissimo sit Nexui,
Decus perennis cantici,
Decus perennis cantici.

---

*With his good gifts which are in us, we
must obey him at all times.*

Dilecte Martyr Numini

based on a translation by Robert Bern '056

O beloved witness to the Divinity,
Meinrad, kindly attune your ear
to the fervent aspirations
of those now singing together.

As once you suffered
blows and a horrible death,
Now crowned with glory
you are clothed in the royal vesture of martyrs.

With Christ going before you as leader,
you would see with disdain
beyond the illusions
which a vain mind would embrace.

Hence you now shine among the stars
more brightly than the sun.
Secure of that reward
for which merit you were killed.

Therefore, please hear the prayers
which beseeching, we pour out
and take up our cause
before the terrible Judge.

Let there be a hymn to the most wonderful Father,
Let there be praise to the greatest Son,
And to their sweetest Unity
A never ending song of praise.

---

*Every exaltation is a kind of pride, which
the Prophet indicates he has shunned.*

History of Saint Meinrad Archabbey

For more than forty years after the death of St. Meinrad, martyr, his hermitage lay deserted. Buildings became ruins and the forest reclaimed the land Meinrad had cleared for his home. But it remained in the hearts of the nearby people a very important religious memory.

In 906, St. Benno, a nobleman and canon from Strasbourg, visited the abandoned hermitage and thought it would make a suitable location for a monastery. He received permission from the government to clear and cultivate the land there, and invited several friends and workers to join him at the newly-established monastery. And so St. Meinrad's beloved chapel to the Blessed Mother, as well as his dwelling itself, were restored and became the foundation for the Abbey of Einsiedeln.

In the mid-tenth century, a large church was built over the cell of St. Meinrad, transforming the humble chapel and dwelling into one shrine—a roofed chapel within the church. The church was dedicated to the Blessed Virgin and the chapel has come to be known as the "Chapel of Graces." Over the succeeding decade, the name of the monastery became known as Einsiedeln, the German equivalent for the word "hermitage."

Through the next ten centuries, Einsiedeln endured many disasters—from fire, to wars, to being

---

If we humble our hearts, the Lord will raise it to heaven.

overtaken by the French. But because of its strong abbots and determination, it survived when many other monasteries did not. As the 1800s progressed, the monks of the the abbey became even more concerned with the political atmosphere of Switzerland. The Swiss government had become hostile to the Catholic Church and had even succeeded in closing some monasteries. The Benedictines at Einsiedeln discussed options for setting up foundation, perhaps in America, to which the monks could flee should the Swiss government exert pressure on them.

As chance would have it, about that time a priest from the Diocese of Vincennes, in Indiana, was traveling through Europe seeking assistance from monasteries. Fr. Joseph Kundek, the vicar-general of the diocese, wanted to find a monastery that would be willing to establish a foundation in southern Indiana and whose German-speaking priests could address the pastoral needs of the ever-growing German Catholic population settling there. Fr. Kundek also hoped the new monastery would be able to educate local men to become priests, thereby increasing the number of clergy in the area. At the Abbey of Einsiedeln, he found an interested ear.

In discussing the possibility of a Benedictine foundation in the new world, the monks of Einsiedeln knew there would be risks. But in late 1852, the monks enthusiastically and unanimously agreed to pursue the investigation of establishing a foundation in America. They decided to investigate the option more closely by sending two priests to scout the suitability of the region.

The second step of humility is that a man loves not his own will nor takes pleasure in the satisfaction of his desires.

Two monks, Fr. Ulrich Christen and Fr. Bede O'Connor, departed for America late that year. It took nearly three months to complete their trip to Indiana. They immediately undertook the work of ministering to the German-speaking Catholics over a very large area. During the course of the next year, after looking at several possible sites around Vincennes, they found a parcel of land in Spencer County, in the southern part of the state, that reminded them so much of their native Switzerland that they bought it. The 160-acre property, owned by a local farmer, was sold to Fr. Ulrich for $2,700, a sizable sum at the time. Additional monks were sent from Einsiedeln to assist in the work of the foundation.

On March 13, 1854, the Benedictine monks of Einsiedeln took possession of their first home in America, a simple three-room log cabin. The bedroom doubled as the chapel. The fledgling foundation was named for St. Meinrad, the martyred monk on whose hermitage their mother Abbey was built. The foundation and cabin were blessed on March 21, the Feast of St. Benedict, with 1,500 faithful standing in pouring rain to participate in the High Mass and dedication.

The first years of the foundation were difficult—filled with poverty, sickness, personal conflict and uncertainty. Because of the need to build new structures and provide for basic necessities, additional debts were taken on. The climate also was difficult for the Swiss monks, with hot, humid summers being especially hard. The

---

We are rightly taught not to do our own will.

monks worked the fields as well as ministered to the people. One monk died from the hard pioneer life; another had to return to Switzerland because of poor health. Yet, on both sides of the Atlantic, the communities tried to look at these challenges with optimism for the future.

As the decade drew to a close and the debts continued to mount, however, Abbot Henry IV Schmid of Einsiedeln questioned whether all the personal and financial investment was worth it. The foundation was going deeper into debt and showed no signs of easily pulling itself out. So, in 1860, Abbot Henry responded to the worsening situation by sending two young monks to Saint Meinrad: Fr. Martin Marty and Fr. Fintan Mundwiler. They were directed to assess the situation, take whatever steps were needed and, if the community at Einsiedeln deemed necessary, to close the foundation. Upon arrival, Fr. Martin was named prior of the community.

After just a short time at Saint Meinrad, Fr. Martin came to see that there was a future for the foundation, provided several needs were addressed promptly. One of the largest concerns was the financial stability of the institution. Among other things, Fr. Martin sold some land surrounding the institution. This effort resulted in two benefits: the funds raised repaid the outstanding loans and a town was formed near the abbey, reminiscent of the village at the foot of Einsiedeln.

---

*We must believe that God is always
with us.*

Within just ten years from the time Fr. Martin arrived at Saint Meinrad, the fate of the foundation had been turned around. Astute management by Fr. Martin and the hard work of the monks resulted in Saint Meinrad having a firm financial footing, so strong in fact the institution was raised to an independent abbey on September 30, 1870. Fr. Martin was chosen as the first abbot.

During this time of establishing itself, Saint Meinrad initiated its program for preparing local men for the priesthood. The first classes, on the secondary school level, began in 1857. By 1861, the monks had added courses in commerce, classics, philosophy and theology. As time went on, the programs focused exclusively on Roman Catholic priesthood formation. Since 1969, however, classes and formation were expanded to address the needs of a changing Church in preparing both priests and lay ministers. And in recent years, a program to form permanent deacons was added. All have used their formation experiences to better minister in their communities, parishes and careers.

The monks of Saint Meinrad undertook other works as well. Certainly for the first century of its existence, the Archabbey was nearly self-sustaining. Food was generated through raising beef and dairy cattle, pork, and poultry, as well as through the orchards and vineyard and many acres of planted crops. The farming operation was closed in the mid-1970s, as it proved to be more costly to maintain the farm than to purchase food from a supplier.

We must be vigilant every hour.

The monks also operated a sandstone quarry near the Monte Cassino Shrine, about a mile from the Archabbey. From that quarry, the monks were able to generate sandstone to construct its buildings here at Saint Meinrad, as well as sell the stone for other church construction throughout the region, and as far south as Florida. Much of the work done in the early years in the quarry was conducted through manual labor of the monks and townspeople and transported by mules and horses.

Rich coal deposits on the Archabbey property allowed the monks to operate a coal mine for many years. In addition to providing fuel to heat the buildings and operate machinery, the monks sold some of the coal to support the seminary formation provided in the Schools.

Perhaps the most far-reaching work of support for the mission of the Schools has been Abbey Press. Since the purchase of a used printing press in the 1860s, Abbey Press has provided printing services to Saint Meinrad and others. However, Abbey Press undertakes its own min-istry—the production and marketing of religious and inspirational cards, books and gifts. Christian families across the country receive catalogs of items that help strengthen their expression of faith. All profits of the Press help support the mission of Saint Meinrad.

But central to all of life on "the Hill" is the devo-tion to prayer. From the moment of the dedication of the simple log cabin until today, the monks gather publicly

---

The faithful must endure everything, even contradiction, for the Lord's sake.

five times each day to raise their voices in praise of God. Even on the day of the most devastating event at Saint Meinrad—the 1887 conflagration that gutted the then recently-completed monastery and chapel—the monks came together in praise and thanksgiving.

The townspeople, students, local religious and other faithful share in the monks' devotion to the Blessed Virgin Mary. For 150 years, individuals have climbed the hill at Monte Cassino in pilgrimage to Mary, the Mother of God. At first, the shrine was a simple lithograph nailed to a tree. This was replaced by a wood chapel, built by the seminary's students and rector. Then, in 1870, the virgin sandstone from the quarry was used in building a shrine to Mary. Public pilgrimages have been held there each May and October since 1932. Yet, private pilgrimages continue daily at Saint Meinrad, each time someone opens his or her heart to prayer "on the Hill."

This sense of prayer, a focusing of one's life on God and how God graces lives, most captures the heritage and importance of Saint Meinrad. Through all its trials and successes; all its works and relaxation; all its preparation of generations of priests, religious and lay Catholics who minister to the Church and those around them; and its emphasis on community and concern for one another; prayer forms a continuous refrain of praise at Saint Meinrad. It is that sense of spirituality that people take with them when they leave, and for which people return, in time, seeking renewal.

Judging himself always guilty on account of his sins, he should consider that he is already at the fearful judgment.

LITURGY OF
THE HOURS

The Psalms recommended herein obviously can be prayed any time of the week, day or night. The person praying the psalms may find some psalms more appropriate for different times of the day. The suggested daily order of psalms presented here follows many traditional arrangements.

---

1. The Two Ways

1 Happy indeed are those
who follow not the counsel of the wicked,
nor linger in the way of sinners
nor sit in the company of scorners,
2 but whose delight is the law of the Lord
and who ponder God's law day and night.

3 They are like a tree that is planted
beside the flowing waters,
that yields its fruit in due season
and whose leaves shall never fade;
and all that they do shall prosper.
4 Not so are the wicked, not so!

For they like winnowed chaff
shall be driven away by the wind.
5 When the wicked are judged they shall not stand,
nor find room among those who are just;
6 for the Lord guards the way of the just
but the way of the wicked leads to doom.

---

*First of all, every time you begin a good
work, you must pray to him most earnestly
to bring it to perfection.*

(62) 63. **Longing for God**

2   O God, you are my God, for you I long;
for you my soul is thirsting.
My body pines for you
like a dry, weary land without water.

3   So I gaze on you in the sanctuary
to see your strength and your glory.

4   For your love is better than life,
my lips will speak your praise.

5   So I will bless you all my life,
in your name I will lift up my hands.

6   My soul shall be filled as with a banquet,
my mouth shall praise you with joy.

7   On my bed I remember you.
On you I muse through the night

8   for you have been my help;
in the shadow of your wings I rejoice.

9   My soul clings to you;
your right hand holds me fast.

10   Those who seek to destroy my life
shall go down to the depths of the earth.

11   They shall be put into the power of the sword
and left as the prey of the jackals.

12   But the king shall rejoice in God;
(all who swear by God shall be blessed,)
for the mouth of liars shall be silenced.

---

*These people fear the Lord, and do not
become elated over their good deeds.*

Daniel 3:57-90
(Prayer of Azariah - Song of the Three Jews)

57   "Bless the Lord, all you works of the Lord;
    sing praise to him and highly exalt him forever.

58   Bless the Lord, you heavens;
    sing praise to him and highly exalt him forever.

59   Bless the Lord, you angels of the Lord;
    sing praise to him and highly exalt him forever.

60   Bless the Lord, all you waters above the heavens;
    sing praise to him and highly exalt him forever.

61   Bless the Lord, all you powers of the Lord;
    sing praise to him and highly exalt him forever.

62   Bless the Lord, sun and moon;
    sing praise to him and highly exalt him forever.

63   Bless the Lord, stars of heaven;
    sing praise to him and highly exalt him forever.

64   "Bless the Lord, all rain and dew;
    sing praise to him and highly exalt him forever.

65   Bless the Lord, all you winds;
    sing praise to him and highly exalt him forever.

66   Bless the Lord, fire and heat;
    sing praise to him and highly exalt him forever.

67   Bless the Lord, winter cold and summer heat;
    sing praise to him and highly exalt him forever.

68   Bless the Lord, dews and falling snow;
    sing praise to him and highly exalt him forever.

Devote yourself often to prayer.

69   Bless the Lord, nights and days;
     sing praise to him and highly exalt him forever.
70   Bless the Lord, light and darkness;
     sing praise to him and highly exalt him forever.
71   Bless the Lord, ice and cold;
     sing praise to him and highly exalt him forever.
72   Bless the Lord, frosts and snows;
     sing praise to him and highly exalt him forever.
73   Bless the Lord, lightnings and clouds;
     sing praise to him and highly exalt him forever.

74   "Let the earth bless the Lord;
     let it sing praise to him and highly exalt him forever.
75   Bless the Lord, mountains and hills;
     sing praise to him and highly exalt him forever.
76   Bless the Lord, all that grows in the ground;
     sing praise to him and highly exalt him forever.
77   Bless the Lord, seas and rivers;
     sing praise to him and highly exalt him forever.
78   Bless the Lord, you springs;
     sing praise to him and highly exalt him forever.
79   Bless the Lord, you whales and all that swim
     in the waters;
     sing praise to him and highly exalt him forever.
80   Bless the Lord, all birds of the air;
     sing praise to him and highly exalt him forever.
81   Bless the Lord, all wild animals and cattle;
     sing praise to him and highly exalt him forever.

---

*The labor of obedience will bring you back
to him from whom you had drifted through
the sloth of disobedience.*

82   "Bless the Lord, all people on earth;
      sing praise to him and highly exalt him forever.
83   Bless the Lord, O Israel;
      sing praise to him and highly exalt him forever.
84   Bless the Lord, you priests of the Lord;
      sing praise to him and highly exalt him forever.
85   Bless the Lord, you servants of the Lord;
      sing praise to him and highly exalt him forever.
86   Bless the Lord, spirits and souls of the righteous;
      sing praise to him and highly exalt him forever.
87   Bless the Lord, you who are holy and humble
      in the heart;
      sing praise to him and highly exalt him forever.
88   "Bless the Lord, Hananiah, Azariah,
      and Mishael;
      sing praise to him and highly exalt him forever.
      For he has rescued us from
      Hades and saved us from
      the power of death,
      and delivered us from the
      midst of the burning fiery furnace;
      from the midst of the fire
      he has delivered us.
89   Give thanks to the Lord, for he is good,
      for his mercy endures forever.
90   All who worship the Lord,
      bless the God of gods,
      sing praise to him
      and give thanks to him,
      for his mercy endures forever."

---

*They judge it is the Lord's power, not their
own, that brings about the good in them.*

(117) 118.   A Processional Song of Praise

1.   Alleluia!

        Give thanks to the Lord who is good,
        for God's love endures for ever.
2   Let the family of Israel say:
        "God's love endures for ever."
3   Let the family of Aaron say:
        "God's love endures for ever."
4   Let those who fear the Lord say:
        "God's love endures for ever."

5   I called to the Lord in my distress;
        God answered and freed me.
6   The Lord is at my side; I do not fear.
        What can mortals do against me?
7   The Lord is at my side as my helper;
        I shall look down on my foes.

8   It is better to take refuge in the Lord
        than to trust in mortals;
9   it is better to take refuge in the Lord
        than to trust in rulers.
10   The nations all encompassed me;
        in the Lord's name I crushed them.
11   They compassed me, compassed me about;
        in the Lord's name I crushed them.

Every day with tears and sighs confess your
past sins to God in prayer.

12   They compassed me about like bees;
      they blazed like a fire among thorns.
      In the Lord's name I crushed them.

13   I was thrust down, thrust down and falling,
      but the Lord was my helper.
14   The Lord is my strength and my song;
      and has been my savior.
15   There are shouts of joy and victory
      in the tents of the just.

      The Lord's right hand has triumphed;
16   God's right hand raised me.
      The Lord's right hand has triumphed;
17   I shall not die, I shall live
      and recount God's deeds.
18   I was punished, I was punished by the Lord,
      but not doomed to die.

19   Open to me the gates of holiness:
      I will enter and give thanks.
20   This is the Lord's own gate
      where the just may enter.
21   I will thank you for you have answered
      and you are my savior.

22   The stone which the builders rejected
      has become the corner stone.

---

*But as we progress in this way of life and
in faith, we shall run on the path of God's
commandments.*

23 This is the work of the Lord,
  a marvel in our eyes.
24 This day was made by the Lord;
  we rejoice and are glad.

25 O Lord, grant us salvation;
  O Lord, grant success.
26 Blessed in the name of the Lord
  is he who comes.
  We bless you from the house of the Lord;
27 the Lord God is our light.

  Go forward in procession with branches
  even to the altar.
28 You are my God, I thank you.
  My God, I praise you.
29 Give thanks to the Lord who is good;
  for God's love endures for ever.

See how the Lord in his love shows us the
way of life.

(144) 145.   **Praise of God's Glory**

1   I will give you glory, O God my king,
      I will bless your name for ever.

2.   I will bless you day after day
      and praise your name for ever.

3   You are great, Lord, highly to be praised,
      your greatness cannot be measured.

4   Age to age shall proclaim your works,
      shall declare your mighty deeds,

5   shall speak of your splendor and glory,
      tell the tale of your wonderful works.

6   They will speak of your terrible deeds,
      recount your greatness and might.

7   They will recall your abundant goodness;
      age to age shall ring out your justice.

8   You are kind and full of compassion,
      slow to anger, abounding in love.

9   How good you are, Lord, to all,
      compassionate to all your creatures.

10   All your creatures shall thank you, O Lord,
      and your friends shall repeat their blessing.

11   They shall speak of the glory of your reign
      and declare your might, O God,

---

*The third step of humility is that a man
submits to his superior in all obedience for
the love of God.*

12   to make known to all your mighty deeds
and the glorious splendor of your reign.

13   Yours is an everlasting kingdom;
your rule lasts from age to age.

you are faithful in all your words
and loving in all your deeds.

14   You support all those who are falling
and raise up all who are bowed down.

15   The eyes of all creatures look to you
and you give them their food in due season.

16   You open wide your hand,
grant the desires of all who live.

17   You are just in all your ways
and loving in all your deeds.

18   You are close to all who call you,
who call on you from their hearts.

19   you grant the desires of those who fear you,
you hear their cry and you save them.

20   Lord, you protect all who love you;
but the wicked you will utterly destroy.

21   Let me speak your praise, O Lord,
let all peoples bless your holy name
for ever, for ages unending.

He must constantly remember everything
God has commanded.

5. Morning Prayer

2   To my words give ear, O Lord,
    give heed to my groaning.

3   Attend to the sound of my cries,
    my King and my God.

4   It is you whom I invoke, O Lord.
    In the morning you hear me;
    in the morning I offer you my prayer,
    watching and waiting.

5   You are no God who loves evil;
    no sinner is your guest.

6   The boastful shall not stand their ground
    before your face.

7   You hate all who do evil;
    you destroy all who lie.
    Deceitful and bloodthirsty people
    are hateful to you, Lord.

8   But I through the greatness of your love
    have access to your house.
    I bow down before your holy temple,
    filled with awe.

*All who despise God will burn in hell for
their sins, and all who fear God have
everlasting life awaiting them.*

9   Lead me, Lord, in your justice,
because of those who lie in wait;
make clear your way before me.

10   No truth can be found in their mouths,
their heart is all mischief,
their throat a wide-open grave,
all honey their speech.

11   Declare them guilty, O God.
Let them fail in their designs.
Drive them out for their many offenses,
for they have defied you.

12   All those you protect shall be glad
and ring out their joy.
You shelter them; in you they rejoice,
those who love your name.

13   Lord, it is you who bless the upright:
you surround them with favor as with a shield.

---

*His actions everywhere are in God's sight
and are reported by angels at every hour.*

6.   **A Prayer in Time of Need**

2   Lord, do not reprove me in your anger;
        punish me not, in your rage.
3   Have mercy on me, Lord, I have no strength;
        Lord, heal me, my body is racked,
4   my soul is racked with pain.

        But you, O Lord...how long?
5   Return, Lord, rescue my soul.
        Save me in your merciful love;
6   for in death no one remembers you;
        from the grave, who can give you praise?

7   I am exhausted with my groaning;
        every night I drench my pillow with tears;
        I soak my bed with weeping.
8   My eye wastes away with grief;
        I have grown old surrounded by my foes.

9   Leave me, all you who do evil,
        for the Lord has heard my weeping.
10   The Lord has heard my plea,
        the Lord will accept my prayer.
11   All my foes will retire in confusion,
        foiled and suddenly confounded.

Let us open our eyes to the light
that comes from God, and our ears to
the voice from heaven.

(18) 19. Praise for the Lord, Creator of All

2   The heavens proclaim the glory of God,
     and the firmament shows forth the work of God's hands.

3   Day unto day takes up the story
     and night unto night makes known the message.

4   No speech, no word, no voice is heard
5   yet their span extends through all the earth,
     their words to the utmost bounds of the world.

     There God has placed a tent for the sun;
6   it comes forth like a bridegroom coming from his tent,
     rejoices like a champion to run its course.
7   At the end of the sky is the rising of the sun;
     to the furthest end of the sky is its course.
     There is nothing concealed from its burning heat.

8   The law of the Lord is perfect,
     it revives the soul.
     The rule of the Lord is to be trusted,
     it gives wisdom to the simple.

9   The precepts of the Lord are right,
     they gladden the heart.
     The command of the Lord is clear,
     it gives light to the eyes.

---

*...There is a wicked zeal of bitterness which
separates from God and leads to hell.*

10   The fear of the Lord is holy,
        abiding for ever.
        The decrees of the Lord are truth
        and all of them just.

11   They are more to be desired than gold,
        than the purest of gold
        and sweeter are they than honey,
        than honey from the comb.

12   So in them your servant finds instruction;
        great reward is in their keeping.
13   But can we discern all our errors?
        From hidden faults acquit us.

14   From presumption restrain your servant
        and let it not rule me.
        Then shall I be blameless,
        clean from grave sin.

15   May the spoken words of my mouth,
        the thoughts of my heart,
        win favor in your sight, O Lord,
        my rescuer, my rock!

*For the obedience shown to superiors is
given to God, as he himself said: Whoever
listens to you, listens to me.*

(15) 16. True Happiness

1   Preserve me, God, I take refuge in you.
2   I say to you Lord: "You are my God.
        My happiness lies in you alone."

3   You have put into my heart a marvelous love
        for the faithful ones who dwell in your land.
4   Those who choose other gods increase their sorrows.
        Never will I offer their offerings of blood.
        Never will I take their name upon my lips.

5   O Lord, it is you who are my portion and cup,
        it is you yourself who are my prize.
6   The lot marked out for me is my delight,
        welcome indeed the heritage that falls to me!

7   I will bless you, Lord, you give me counsel,
        and even at night direct my heart.
8   I keep you, Lord, ever in my sight;
        since you are at my right hand, I shall stand firm.

9   And so my heart rejoices, my soul is glad;
        even my body shall rest in safety.
10   For you will not leave my soul among the dead,
        nor let your beloved know decay.

11   You will show me the path of life,
        the fullness of joy in your presence,
        at your right hand happiness for ever.

Change from these evil ways in the future.

(90) 91. **Under the Wing of God's Protection**

1   Those who dwell in the shelter of the Most High
     and abide in the shade of the Almighty
2   say to the Lord: "My refuge,
     my stronghold, my God in whom I trust!"

3   It is God who will free you from the snare
     of the fowler who seeks to destroy you;
4   God will conceal you with his pinions,
     and under his wings you will find refuge.

5   You will not fear the terror of the night
     nor the arrow that flies by day,
6   nor the plague that prowls in the darkness
     nor the scourge that lays waste at noon.

7   A thousand may fall at your side,
     ten thousand fall at your right,
     you, it will never approach;
4c   God's faithfulness is buckler and shield.

8   Your eyes have only to look
     to see how the wicked are repaid,
9   you who have said: "Lord, my refuge!"
     and have made the Most High your dwelling.

Let him recall that he is always seen by
God in heaven.

10	Upon you no evil shall fall, no plague approach where you dwell.
11	For you God has commanded the angels, to keep you in all your ways.
12	They shall bear you upon their hands lest you strike your foot against a stone.
13	On the lion and the viper you will tread and trample the young lion and the dragon.
14	You set your love on me so I will save you, protect you for you know my name.
15	When you call I shall answer: "I am with you," I will save you in distress and give you glory.
16	With length of days I will content you; I shall let you see my saving power.

---

*If we wish to dwell in the tent of this
kingdom, we will never arrive unless we
run there by doing good deeds.*

(9b) 10. A Prayer for Justice

1 Lord, why do you stand afar off
 and hide yourself in times of distress?
2 The poor are devoured by the pride of the wicked;
 they are caught in the schemes that others have made.

3 For the wicked boast of their heart's desires;
 the covetous blaspheme and spurn the Lord.
4 In their pride the wicked say: "God will not punish.
 There is no God." Such are their thoughts.

5 Their path is ever untroubled;
 our judgement is far from their minds.
 Their enemies they regard with contempt.
6 They think: "Never shall we falter:
 misfortune shall never be our lot."

7 Their mouths are full of cursing, guile, oppression;
 mischief and deceit are their food.
8 They lie in wait among the reeds;
 they murder the innocent in secret.

 Their eyes are on the watch for the helpless.
9 They lurk in hiding like lions in their den;
 they lurk in hiding to seize the poor;
 they seize the poor and drag them away.

---

*On arising for the Work of God, they will
quietly encourage each other, for the sleepy
like to make excuses.*

10 They crouch, preparing to spring,
and the helpless fall beneath such strength.

11 They think in their hearts: "God forgets,
God does not look, God does not see."

12 Arise then, Lord, lift up your hand!
O God, do not forget the poor!

13 Why should the wicked spurn the Lord
and think in their hearts: "God will not punish"?

14 But you have seen the trouble and sorrow,
you note it, you take it in hand.
The helpless entrust themselves to you,
for you are the helper of the orphan.

15 Break the power of the wicked and the sinner!
Punish their wickedness till nothing remains!

16 The Lord is king for ever and ever.
The heathen shall perish from the land of the Lord.

17 Lord, you hear the prayer of the poor;
you strengthen their hearts; you turn your ear

18 to protect the rights of the orphan and oppressed
so that those from the earth may strike terror no more.

Hate the urgings of self-will.

(23) 24. **The Lord of Glory**

1   The Lord's is the earth and its fullness,
     the world and all its peoples.
2   It is God who set it on the seas;
     who made it firm on the waters.

3   Who shall climb the mountain of the Lord?
     Who shall stand in God's holy place?
4   Those with clean hands and pure heart,
     who desire not worthless things,
     (who have not sworn so as to deceive their neighbor.)

5   They shall receive blessings from the Lord
     and reward from the God who saves them.
6   These are the ones who seek,
     seek the face of the God of Jacob.
7   O gates, lift high your heads;
     grow higher, ancient doors.
     Let the king of glory enter!

8   Who is the king of glory?
     The Lord, the mighty, the valiant,
     the Lord, the valiant in war.

---

*No one may be disquieted or distressed in
the house of God.*

9   O gates, lift high your heads;
grow higher, ancient doors.
Let the king of glory enter!

10   Who is the king of glory?
The Lord of heavenly armies.
This is the king of glory.

---

*The Lord waits for us daily to translate
into action, as we should, his holy
teachings.*

(36) 37. **Reflections on Good and Evil**

1   Do not fret because of the wicked;
    do not envy those who do evil,

2   for they wither quickly like grass
    and fade like the green of the fields.

3   If you trust in the Lord and do good,
    then you will live in the land and be secure.

4   If you find your delight in the Lord,
    he will grant your heart's desire.

5   Commit your life to the Lord,
    be confident, and God will act,

6   so that your justice breaks forth like the light,
    your cause like the noonday sun.

7   Be still before the Lord and wait in patience;
    do not fret at those who prosper;
    those who make evil plots

14c   to bring down the needy and the poor.

8   Calm your anger and forget your rage;
    do not fret, it only leads to evil.

9   For those who do evil shall perish;
    those waiting for the Lord shall inherit the land.

The fourth step of humility is that in his heart
quietly embraces suffering and endures it
without weakening or seeking escape.

10   A little longer—and the wicked shall have gone.
Look at their homes, they are not there.

11   But the humble shall own the land
and enjoy the fullness of peace.

Above all, let him be humble.

(70) 71. A Prayer in Old Age

1   In you, O Lord, I take refuge;
       let me never be put to shame.
2   In your justice rescue me, free me;
       pay heed to me and save me.

3   Be a rock where I can take refuge,
       a mighty stronghold to save me;
       for you are my rock, my stronghold.
4   Free me from the hand of the wicked,
       from the grip of the unjust, of the oppressor.

5   It is you, O Lord, who are my hope,
       my trust, O Lord, since my youth.
6   On you I have leaned from my birth;
       from my mother's womb you have been my help.
       My hope has always been in you.

7   My fate has filled many with awe
       but you are my strong refuge.
8   My lips are filled with your praise,
       with your glory all the day long.
9   Do not reject me now that I am old;
       when my strength fails do not forsake me.

10   For my enemies are speaking about me;
       those who watch me take counsel together.

---

*Do not aspire to be called holy before you
really are, but first be holy that you may
more truly be called so.*

11 They say that God has forsaken me,
   they can seize me and no one will save me.
12 O God, do not stay far off:
   my God, make haste to help me!

13 Let them be put to shame and destroyed,
   all those who seek my life.
   Let them be covered with shame and confusion,
   all those who seek to harm me.

14 But as for me, I will always hope
   and praise you more and more.
15 My lips will tell of your justice
   and day by day of your help
   (though I can never tell it all).

16 Lord, I will declare your mighty deeds,
   proclaiming your justice, yours alone.
17 O God, you have taught me from my youth
   and I proclaim your wonders still.

18 Now that I am old and grey-headed,
   do not forsake me, God.
   Let me tell of your power to all ages,
   praise your strength
19 and justice to the skies,
   tell of you who have worked such wonders.
   O God, who is like you?

He must show every care and concern for
the sick, children, guests and the poor.

20   You have burdened me with bitter troubles
     but you will give me back my life.
     You will raise me from the depths of the earth;
21   You will exalt me and console me again.

22   So I will give you thanks on the lyre
     for your faithful love, my God.
     To you will I sing with the harp,
     to you, the Holy One of Israel.
23   When I sing to you my lips shall rejoice
     and my soul, which you have redeemed.

24   And all the day long my tongue
     shall tell the tale of your justice:
     for they are put to shame and disgraced,
     all those who seek to harm me.

What is not possible to us by nature,
let us ask the Lord to supply by the help
of his grace.

(66) 67. A Harvest Song

2   O God, be gracious and bless us
and let your face shed its light upon us.

3   So will your ways be known upon earth
and all nations learn your saving help.

4   Let the peoples praise you, O God;
let all the peoples praise you.

5   Let the nations be glad and exult
for you rule the world with justice.
With fairness you rule the peoples,
you guide the nations on earth.

6   Let the peoples praise you, O God;
let all peoples praise you.

7   The earth has yielded its fruit
for God, our God, has blessed us.

8   May God still give us blessing
till the ends of the earth stand in awe.

Let the peoples praise you, O God;
let all the peoples praise you.

---

*Whoever needs less should thank God and
not be distressed.*

(26) 27. **Trust in Time of Affliction**

1   The Lord is my light and my help;
whom shall I fear?
The Lord is the stronghold of my life;
before whom shall I shrink?

2   When evildoers draw near
to devour my flesh,
it is they, my enemies and foes,
who stumble and fall.

3   Though an army encamp against me
my heart would not fear.
Though war break out against me
even then would I trust.

4   There is one thing I ask of the Lord,
for this I long,
to live in the house of the Lord,
all the days of my life,
to savor the sweetness of the Lord,
to behold his temple.

5   For God makes me safe in his tent
in the day of evil.
God hides me in the shelter of his tent,
on a rock I am secure.

Live by God's commandments every day.

6   And now my head shall be raised
     above my foes who surround me
     and I shall offer within God's tent
     a sacrifice of joy.

     I will sing and make music for the Lord.

7   O Lord, hear my voice when I call;
     have mercy and answer.
8   Of you my heart has spoken:
     "Seek God's face."

     It is your face, O Lord, that I seek;
9   hide not your face.
     Dismiss not your servant in anger;
     you have been my help.

     Do not abandon or forsake me,
     O God my help!
10   Though father and mother forsake me,
     the Lord will receive me.

11   Instruct me, Lord, in your way;
     on an even path lead me.
     When they lie in ambush
12   protect me from my enemies' greed.
     False witnesses rise against me,
     breathing out fury.

---

*First and foremost, there must be no word
or sign of the evil of grumbling.*

13   I am sure I shall see the Lord's goodness
in the land of the living.

14   In the Lord, hold firm and take heart.
Hope in the Lord!

*We must run and do now what will profit
us forever.*

(142) 143.   A Prayer in Desolation: Seventh Psalm of Repentance

1   Lord, listen to my prayer,
        turn your ear to my appeal.
        You are faithful, you are just; give answer.
2   Do not call your servant to judgement
        for no one is just in your sight.

3   The enemy pursues my soul;
        has crushed my life to the ground;
        has made me dwell in the darkness
        like the dead, long forgotten.
4   Therefore my spirit fails;
        my heart is numb within me.

5   I remember the days that are past;
        I ponder all your works,
        I muse on what your hand has wrought
6   and to you I stretch out my hands.
        Like a parched land my soul thirsts for you.

7   Lord, make haste and answer;
        for my spirit fails within me.
        Do not hide your face
        lest I become like those in the grave.

---

*Do not be daunted immediately by fear
and run away from the road that leads
to salvation.*

8   In the morning let me know your love
       for I put my trust in you.
       Make me know the way I should walk;
       to you I lift up my soul.

9   Rescue me, Lord, from my enemies;
       I have fled to you for refuge.
10   Teach me to do your will
       for you, O Lord, are my God.
       Let your good spirit guide me
       in ways that are level and smooth.

11   For your name's sake, Lord, save my life;
       in your justice save my soul from distress.
12   In your love make an end of my foes;
       destroy all those who oppress me
       for I am your servant, O Lord.

The fifth step of humility is that a man
does not conceal from his abbot any
sinful thoughts.

(38) 39. No Abiding City

2   I said: "I will be watchful of my ways
for fear I should sin with my tongue.
I will put a curb on my lips
when the wicked stand before me."

3   I was mute, silent and still.
Their prosperity stirred my grief.

4   My heart was burning within me.
At the thought of it, the fire blazed up
and my tongue burst into speech:

5   "O Lord, you have shown me my end,
how short is the length of my days.
Now I know how fleeting is my life.

6   You have given me a short span of days;
my life is as nothing in your sight.
A mere breath, the one who stood so firm;

7   a mere shadow, the one who passes by;
a mere breath, the hoarded riches,
and who will take them, no one knows.

8   And now, Lord, what is there to wait for?
In you rests all my hope.

9   Set me free from all my sins;
do not make me the taunt of the fool.

10   I was silent, not opening my lips,
because this was all your doing.

The brothers should serve one another.

11   Take away your scourge from me.
     I am crushed by the blows of your hand.
12   You punish our sins and correct us;
     like a moth you devour all we treasure.
     Human life is not more than a breath;
13   O Lord, hear my prayer.
     O Lord, turn your ear to my cry.
     Do not be deaf to my tears.
     In your house I am a passing guest,
     a pilgrim, like all my ancestors.
14   Look away that I may breathe again
     before I depart to be no more.

Whoever needs more should feel humble
because of his weakness, not self-important
because of the kindness shown him.

(138) 139. God's Knowledge and Care

1   O Lord, you search me and you know me,
2   you know my resting and my rising,
    you discern my purpose from afar.
3   You mark when I walk or lie down,
    all my ways lie open to you.

4   Before ever a word is on my tongue
    you know it, O Lord, through and through.
5   Behind and before you besiege me,
    your hand ever laid upon me.
6   Too wonderful for me, this knowledge,
    too high, beyond my reach.

7   O where can I go from your spirit,
    or where can I flee from your face?
8   If I climb the heavens, you are there.
    If I lie in the grave, you are there.

9   If I take the wings of the dawn
    and dwell at the sea's furthest end,
10   even there your hand would lead me,
    your right hand would hold me fast.

11   If I say: "Let the darkness hide me
    and the light around me be night,"
12   even darkness is not dark for you
    and the night is as clear as the day.

---

*Harbor neither hatred nor jealousy of
anyone, and do nothing out of envy.*

13   For it was you who created my being,
    knit me together in my mother's womb.
14   I thank you for the wonder of my being,
    for the wonders of all your creation.

    Already you knew my soul,
15   my body held no secret from you
    when I was being fashioned in secret
    and moulded in the depths of the earth.

16   Your eyes saw all my actions,
    they were all of them written in your book;
    every one of my days was decreed
    before one of them came into being.

17   To me, how mysterious your thoughts,
    the sum of them not to be numbered!
18   If I count them, they are more than the sand;
    to finish, I must be eternal, like you.

19   O God, that you would slay the wicked!
    Keep away from me, violent hands!
20   With deceit they rebel against you
    and set your designs at naught.

21   Do I not hate those who hate you,
    abhor those who rise against you?
22   I hate them with a perfect hate
    and they are foes to me.

---

*Let the sick on their part bear in mind
that they are served out of honor for God.*

23   O search me, God, and know my heart.
       O test me and know my thoughts.
24   See that I follow not the wrong path
       and lead me in the path of life eternal.

For nothing is so inconsistent with the life
of any Christian as overindulgence.

(133) 134. Prayer at Nighttime: A Pilgrimage Song

1   O come, bless the Lord,
       all you who serve the Lord,
       who stand in the house of the Lord,
       in the courts of the house of our God.

2   Lift up your hands to the holy place
       and bless the Lord through the night.

3   May the Lord bless you from Zion,
       God who made both heaven and earth.

Rid your heart of all deceit.

Deliver us, Lord,
from every evil,
and grant us peace
in our day.
In your mercy,
keep us free from sin,
and protect us from all anxiety

as we WAIT
IN JOYFUL
HOPE for the
coming of
Our Savior
Jesus Christ

THURSDAY

(24) 25. A Prayer for Guidance and Protection

1	To you, O Lord, I lift up my soul.
2	My God, I trust you, let me not be disappointed;
	do not let my enemies triumph.
3	Those who hope in you shall not be disappointed,
	but only those who wantonly break faith.

4	Lord, make me know your ways.
	Lord, teach me your paths.
5	Make me walk in your truth, and teach me,
	for you are God my savior.

	In you I hope all the day long
7c	because of your goodness, O Lord.
6	Remember your mercy, Lord,
	and the love you have shown from of old.
7	Do not remember the sins of my youth.
	In your love remember me.

8	The Lord is good and upright.
	Showing the path to those who stray,
9	guiding the humble in the right path,
	and teaching the way to the poor.

10	God's ways are steadfastness and truth
	for those faithful to the covenant decrees
11	Lord, for the sake of your name
	forgive my guilt, for it is great.

Do not love quarreling; shun arrogance.

12	Those who revere the Lord
	will be shown the path they should choose.
13	Their souls will live in happiness
	and their children shall possess the land.
14	The Lord's friendship is for the God-fearing;
	and the covenant is revealed to them.
15	My eyes are always on the Lord,
	who will rescue my feet from the snare.
16	Turn to me and have mercy
	for I am lonely and poor.
17	Relieve the anguish of my heart
	and set me free from my distress.
18	See my affliction and my toil
	and take all my sins away.
19	See how many are my foes,
	how violent their hatred for me.
20	Preserve my life and rescue me.
	Do not disappoint me, you are my refuge.
21	May innocence and uprightness protect me,
	for my hope is in you, O Lord.
22	Redeem Israel, O God, from all its distress.

Indeed, nothing is to be preferred to the
Work of God.

(102) 103. **Praise of God's Mercy and Love**

1   My soul, give thanks to the Lord,
    all my being, bless God's holy name.
2   My soul, give thanks to the Lord
    and never forget all God's blessings.

3   It is God who forgives all your guilt,
    who heals every one of your ills,
4   who redeems your life from the grave,
    who crowns you with love and compassion,
5   who fills your life with good things,
    renewing your youth like an eagle's.

6   The Lord does deeds of justice,
    gives judgement for all who are oppressed
7   the Lord's ways were made known to Moses;
    the Lord's deeds to Israel's children.

8   The Lord is compassion and love,
    slow to anger and rich in mercy.
9   The Lord will not always chide,
    will not be angry forever.
10 God does not treat us according to our sins
    nor repay us according to our faults.

11 For as the heavens are high above the earth
    so strong is God's love for the God-fearing;
12 As far as the east is from the west
    so far does he remove our sins.

Respect the elders and love the young.

13   As parents have compassion on their children,
      the Lord has pity on those who are God-fearing
14   for he knows of what we are made,
      and remembers that we are dust.

15   As for us, our days are like grass;
      we flower like the flower of the field;
16   the wind blows and we are gone
      and our place never sees us again.

17   But the love of the Lord is everlasting
      upon those who fear the Lord.
      God's justice reaches out to children's children
18   when they keep his covenant in truth,
      when they keep his will in their mind.

19   The Lord has set his throne in heaven
      and his kingdom rules over all.
20   Give thanks to the Lord, all you angels,
      mighty in power, fulfilling God's word,
      who heed the voice of that word.

21   Give thanks to the Lord, all you hosts,
      you servants who do God's will.
22   Give thanks to the Lord, all his works,
      in every place where God rules.
      My soul, give thanks to the Lord!

Idleness is the enemy of the soul.

(22) 23. **God, Shepherd and Host**

1   Lord, you are my shepherd;
      there is nothing I shall want.
2   Fresh and green are the pastures
      where you give me repose.
      Near restful waters you lead me,
3   to revive my drooping spirit.

      You guide me along the right path;
      You are true to your name.
4   If I should walk in the valley of darkness
      no evil would I fear.
      You are there with your crook and your staff;
      with these you give me comfort.

5   You have prepared a banquet for me
      in the sight of my foes.
      My head you have anointed with oil;
      my cup is overflowing.

6   Surely goodness and kindness shall follow me
      all the days of my life.
      In the Lord's own house shall I dwell
      for ever and ever.

Place your hope in God alone.

(89) 90. God's Eternity and the Shortness of Life

1   O Lord, you have been our refuge
      from one generation to the next.

2   Before the mountains were born
      or the earth or the world brought forth,
      you are God, without beginning or end.

3   You turn us back into dust
      and say: "Go back, children of the earth."

4   To your eyes a thousand years
      are like yesterday, come and gone,
      no more than a watch in the night.

5   You sweep us away like a dream,
      like grass which springs up in the morning.

6   In the morning it springs up and flowers;
      by evening it withers and fades.

7   So we are destroyed in your anger,
      struck with terror in your fury.

8   Our guilt lies open before you,
      our secrets in the light of your face.

9   All our days pass away in your anger.
      Our life is over like a sigh.

10   Our span is seventy years,
      or eighty for those who are strong.

---

*Great care and concern are to be shown in
receiving poor people and pilgrims.*

And most of these are emptiness and pain.
They pass swiftly and we are gone.

11 Who understands the power of your anger
and fears the strength of your fury?

12 Make us know the shortness of our life
that we may gain wisdom of the heart.

13 Lord, relent! Is your anger for ever?
Show pity to your servants.

14 In the morning, fill us with your love;
we shall exult and rejoice all our days.

15 Give us joy to balance our affliction
for the years when we knew misfortune.

16 Show forth your work to your servants;
let your glory shine on their children.

17 Let the favor of the Lord be upon us;
give success to the work of our hands
(give success to the work of our hands).

---

*He must be chaste, temperate and
merciful.*

(129) 130. **A Prayer of Repentance and Trust: Sixth Psalm of Repentance**

1 Out of the depths I cry to you, O Lord,
2 Lord, hear my voice!
O let your ears be attentive
to the voice of my pleading.

3 If you, O Lord, should mark our guilt,
Lord, who would survive?
4 But with you is found forgiveness:
for this we revere you.

5 My soul is waiting for the Lord.
I count on God's word.
6 My soul is longing for the Lord
more than those who watch for daybreak.
(Let the watchers count on daybreak
7 and Israel on the Lord.)

Because with the Lord there is mercy
and fullness of redemption,
8 Israel indeed God will redeem
from all its iniquity.

---

*The sixth step of humility is that a monk is
content with the lowest and most menial
treatment.*

FRIDAY

(50) 51. A Prayer of Contrition: Fourth Psalm of Repentance

3   Have mercy on me, God, in your kindness.
       In your compassion blot out my offense.
4   O wash me more and more from my guilt
       and cleanse me from my sin.

5   My offenses truly I know them;
       my sin is always before me.
6   Against you, you alone, have I sinned;
       what is evil in your sight I have done.

       That you may be justified when you give sentence
       and be without reproach when you judge,
7   O see, in guilt I was born,
       a sinner was I conceived.

8   Indeed you love truth in the heart;
       then in the secret of my heart teach me wisdom.
9   O purify me, then I shall be clean;
       O wash me, I shall be whiter than snow.

10   Make me hear rejoicing and gladness
       that the bones you have crushed may revive.
       From my sins turn away your face
       and blot out all my guilt.

---

*He should always let mercy triumph over
judgment so that he too may win mercy.*

12   A pure heart create for me, O God,
       put a steadfast spirit within me.
13   Do not cast me away from your presence,
       nor deprive me of your holy spirit.

14   Give me again the joy of your help;
       with a spirit of fervor sustain me,
       that I may teach transgressors your ways
       and sinners may return to you.

16   O rescue me, God, my helper,
       and my tongue shall ring out your goodness.
17   O Lord, open my lips
       and my mouth shall declare your praise.

18   For in sacrifice you take no delight,
       burnt offering from me you would refuse;
19   my sacrifice, a contrite spirit,
       a humbled, contrite heart you will not spurn.

20   In your goodness, show favor to Zion;
       rebuild the walls of Jerusalem.
21   Then you will be pleased with lawful sacrifice,
       (burnt offerings wholly consumed),
       then you will be offered young bulls on your altar.

---

*Renounce yourself in order
to follow Christ.*

(45) 46. **God Is with Us**

2   God is for us a refuge and strength,
       a helper close at hand, in time of distress,
3   so we shall not fear though the earth should rock,
       though the mountains fall into the depths of the sea;
4   even though its waters rage and foam,
       even though the mountains be shaken by its waves.

       The Lord of hosts is with us;
       The God of Jacob is our stronghold.

5   The waters of a river give joy to God's city,
       the holy place where the Most High dwells.
6   God is within, it cannot be shaken;
       God will help it at the dawning of the day.
7   Nations are in tumult, kingdoms are shaken;
       God's voice roars forth, the earth shrinks away.

8   The Lord of hosts is with us;
       the God of Jacob is our stronghold.

9   Come, consider the works of the Lord,
       the redoubtable deeds God has done on the earth:
10   putting an end to wars across the earth;
       breaking the bow, snapping the spear,
       [burning the shields with fire.]

He must hate faults but love the brothers.

11   "Be still and know that I am God,
        supreme among the nations, supreme on the earth!"

12   The Lord of hosts is with us;
        the God of Jacob is our stronghold.

---

*If you have a dispute with someone, make
peace with him before the sun goes down.*

(121) 122. **In Praise of Jerusalem: A Pilgrimage Song**

1 I rejoiced when I heard them say:
   "Let us go to God's house."
2 And now our feet are standing
   within your gates, O Jerusalem.

3 Jerusalem is built as a city
   strongly compact.
4 It is there that the tribes go up,
   the tribes of the Lord.

   For Israel's law it is,
   there to praise the Lord's name.
5 There were set the thrones of judgement
   of the house of David.

6 For the peace of Jerusalem pray:
   "Peace be to your homes!
7 May peace reign in your walls,
   in your palaces, peace!"

8 For love of my family and friends
   I say: "Peace upon you."
9 For love of the house of the Lord
   I will ask for your good.

---

*There is good zeal which separates from
evil and leads to God and everlasting life.*

(21) 22. **The Just One in Distress**

2   My God, my God, why have you forsaken me?
        You are far from my plea and the cry of my distress.

3   O my God, I call by day and you give no reply;
        I call by night and I find no peace.

4   Yet you, O God, are holy,
        enthroned on the praises of Israel.

5   In you our forebears put their trust;
        they trusted and you set them free.

6   When they cried to you, they escaped.
        In you they trusted and never in vain.

7   But I am a worm and no man,
        the butt of all, laughing-stock of the people.

8   All who see me deride me.
        They curl their lips, they toss their heads.

9   "He trusted in the Lord, let him save him,
        and release him if this is his friend."

10   Yes, it was you who took me from the womb,
        entrusted me to my mother's breast.

11   To you I was committed from my birth,
        from my mother's womb you have been my God.

12   Do not leave me alone in my distress;
        Come close, there is none else to help.

Never lose hope in God's mercy.

13   Many bulls have surrounded me,
       fierce bulls of Bashan close me in.
14   Against me they open wide their jaws,
       like lions, rending and roaring.

15   Like water I am poured out,
       disjointed are all my bones.
       My heart has become like wax,
       it is melted within my breast.
16   Parched as burnt clay is my throat,
       my tongue cleaves to my jaws.

17   Many dogs have surrounded me,
       a band of the wicked beset me.
       They tear holes in my hands and my feet
16c   and lay me in the dust of death.

18   I can count every one of my bones.
       These people stare at me and gloat;
19   they divide my clothing among them.
       They cast lots for my robe.

20   O Lord, do not leave me alone,
       my strength, make haste to help me!
21   Rescue my soul from the sword,
       my life from the grip of these dogs.
22   Save my life from the jaws of these lions,
       my soul from the horns of these oxen.

---

*Supporting with the greatest patience one
another's weaknesses of body or behavior.*

23 I will tell of your name to my people
  and praise you where they are assembled.
24 "You who fear the Lord give praise;
  all children of Jacob, give glory.
  Revere God, children of Israel.

25 For God has never despised
  nor scorned the poverty of the poor,
  nor looked away from them,
  but has heard the poor when they cried."

26 You are my praise in the great assembly.
  My vows I will pay before those who fear God.
27 The poor shall eat and shall have their fill.
  Those who seek the Lord shall praise the Lord.
  May their hearts live for ever and ever!

28 All the earth shall remember and return to the Lord,
  all families of the nations shall bow down in awe;
29 for the kingdom is the Lord's, who is ruler of all.
30 They shall bow down in awe, all the mighty of the earth,
  all who must die and go down to the dust.

  My soul shall live for God
31 and my children too shall serve.
  they shall tell of the Lord to generations yet to come;
32 declare to those unborn, the faithfulness of God.
  "These things the Lord has done."

No one is to pursue what he judges better
for himself.

(130) 131. The Peaceful Heart: A Pilgrimage Song

1   O Lord, my heart is not proud
     nor haughty my eyes.
     I have not gone after things too great
     nor marvels beyond me.

2   Truly I have set my soul
     in silence and peace.
     A weaned child on its mother's breast,
     even so is my soul.

3   O Israel, hope in the Lord
     both now and forever.

---

*They are to pray together and thus be
united in peace.*

8. **Divine Glory and Human Dignity**

2   How great is your name, O Lord our God,
through all the earth!

Your majesty is praised above the heavens;
3   on the lips of children and of babes
you have found praise to foil your enemy,
to silence the foe and the rebel.

4   When I see the heavens, the work of your hands,
the moon and the stars which you arranged,
5   what are we that you should keep us in mind,
mere mortals that you care for us?

6   Yet you have made us little less than gods;
and crowned us with glory and honor,
7   you gave us power over the work of your hands,
put all things under our feet.

8   All of them, sheep and cattle,
yes, even the savage beasts,
9   birds of the air, and fish
that make their way through the waters.

10   How great is your name, O Lord our God,
through all the earth!

---

*It is love that impels them to pursue
everlasting life.*

(16) 17. **A Prayer of an Innocent Person**

1   Lord, hear a cause that is just,
     pay heed to my cry.
     Turn your ear to my prayer,
     no deceit is on my lips.

2   From you may my judgement come forth.
     Your eyes discern the truth.

3   You search my heart, you visit me by night.
     You test me and you find in me no wrong.
4   My words are not sinful like human words.

     I keep from violence because of your word,
5   I kept my feet firmly in your paths;
     there was no faltering in my steps.

6   I am here and I call, you will hear me, O God.
     Turn your ear to me; hear my words.
7   Display your great love, you whose right hand saves
     your friends from those who rebel against them.

8   Guard me as the apple of your eye.
     Hide me in the shadow of your wings.
9   from the violent attack of the wicked.

     My foes encircle me with deadly intent.
10   Their hearts tight shut, their mouths speak proudly.

Devote yourself often to prayer.

11   They advance against me, and now they surround
        me.

        Their eyes are watching to strike me to the ground,
12   as though they were lions ready to claw
        or like some young lion crouched in hiding.

13   Lord, arise, confront them, strike them down!
        Let your sword rescue me from the wicked;
14   let your hand, O Lord, rescue me,
        from those whose reward is in this present life.

        You give them their fill of your treasures;
        they rejoice in abundance of offspring
        and leave their wealth to their children.

15   As for me, in my justice I shall see your face
        and be filled, when I awake, with the sight of your
        glory.

What passage of the inspired books of the
Old and New Testaments is not the truest
of guides for human life?

(127) 128.   The Blessings of Home: A Pilgrimage Song

1   O blessed are you who fear the Lord
     and walk in God's ways!
2   By the labor of your hands you shall eat.
     You will be happy and prosper;
3   your wife like a fruitful vine
     in the heart of your house;
     your children like shoots of the olive,
     around your table.

4   Indeed thus shall be blessed
     those who fear the Lord.
5   May the Lord bless you from Zion
5c   all the days of your life!
6   May you see your children's children
5b   in a happy Jerusalem!

     On Israel, peace!

*The Lord will by the Holy Spirit graciously
manifest in his workman now cleansed
of vices and sins.*

Whenever
you begin a good work
PRAY TO GOD
most earnestly
to bring it to
perfection

RULE OF ST. BENEDICT : PROLOGUE

PSALMS
AND
CANTICLES

4. Night Prayer

2   When I call, answer me, O God of justice;
from anguish you released me,
have mercy and hear me!

3   You rebels, how long will your hearts be closed,
will you love what is futile and seek what is false?

4   It is the Lord who grants favors
to those who are merciful;
the Lord hears me whenever I call.

5   Tremble; do not sin: ponder on your bed and be still.
6   Make justice your sacrifice and trust in the Lord.

7   "What can bring us happiness?" many say.
Lift up the light of your face on us, O Lord.

8   You have put into my heart a greater joy
than they have from abundance
of corn and new wine.

9   I will lie down in peace and sleep comes at once
for you alone, Lord, make me dwell in safety.

---

*You must relieve the lot of the poor, clothe
the naked, visit the sick, and bury the dead.*

(31) 32.   The Joy of Being Forgiven

1   Happy those whose offense is forgiven,
        whose sin is remitted.
2   O happy those to whom the Lord
        imputes no guilt,
        in whose spirit is no guile.

3   I kept it secret and my frame was wasted.
        I groaned all day long,
4   for night and day your hand
        was heavy upon me.
        Indeed my strength was dried up
        as by the summer's heat.

5   But now I have acknowledged my sins;
        my guilt I did not hide.
        I said: "I will confess
        my offense to the Lord."
        And you, Lord, have forgiven
        the guilt of my sin.

6   So let faithful people pray to you
        in time of need.
        The floods of water may reach high
        but they shall stand secure.
7   You are my hiding place, O Lord;
        you save me from distress.
        (You surround me with cries of deliverance.)

They should each try to be the first to show
respect to the other.

8   I will instruct you and teach you
the way you should go;
I will give you counsel
with my eye upon you.

9   Be not like horse and mule, unintelligent,
needing bridle and bit,
else they will not approach you.

10   Many sorrows have the wicked,
but those who trust in the Lord
are surrounded with loving mercy.

11   Rejoice, rejoice in the Lord,
exult, you just!
O Come, ring out your joy,
all you upright of heart.

---

*Go to help the troubled and console
the sorrowing.*

(54) 55. A Prayer in Betrayal and Distress

2   O God, listen to my prayer,
       do not hide from my pleading,
3   attend to me and reply;
       with my cares, I cannot rest.

       I tremble
4   at the shouts of the foe,
       at the cries of the wicked;
       for they bring down evil upon me.
       They assail me with fury.

5   My heart is stricken within me,
       death's terror is on me,
6   trembling and fear fall upon me
       and horror overwhelms me.

7   O that I had wings like a dove
       to fly away and be at rest.
8   So I would escape far away
       and take refuge in the desert.

9   I would hasten to find a shelter
       from the raging wind,
       from the destructive storm, O Lord,
10   and from their plotting tongues.
       For I can see nothing but violence
       and strife in the city.

---

*We must know that God regards our
purity of heart and tears of compunction,
not our many words.*

11   Night and day they patrol
high on the city walls.

It is full of wickedness and evil,
12   it is full of sin.
Its streets are never free
from tyranny and deceit.

13   If this had been done by an enemy
then I could bear it.
If a rival had risen against me,
then I could hide.

14   But it is you, my own companion,
my intimate friend!
15   (How close was the friendship between us.)
We walked together in harmony
in the house of God.

16   May death fall suddenly upon them!
Let them go to the grave;
for wickedness dwells in their homes
and deep in their hearts.

17   As for me, I will cry to God
and the Lord will save me.
18   Evening, morning and at noon
I will cry and lament.

---

*Similarly we read, consent merits
punishment; constraint wins a crown.*

19	God will deliver my soul in peace
	in the attack against me;
	for those who fight me are many,
18c	but God hears my voice.

20	God will hear and will humble them,
	the eternal judge;
	for they will not amend their ways.
	They have no fear of God.

21	My companion has turned against me
	has broken our pact,
22	with speech softer than butter,
	with a heart set on war,
	with words smoother than oil,
	though they are naked swords.

23	Entrust your cares to the Lord
	to God who supports you.
	The Lord will never allow
	the just one to stumble.

24	But you, O God, will bring them down
	to the pit of death.
	The bloodthirsty and the deceitful
	shall not live half their lives.

O Lord, I will trust in you.

---

*Furthermore, the disciples' obedience
must be given gladly, for God loves a
cheerful giver.*

(99) 100. Praise to God, Creator and Shepherd

1   Cry out with joy to the Lord, all the earth.
2   Serve the Lord with gladness.
     Come before God, singing for joy.

3   Know that the Lord is God,
     Our Maker, to whom we belong.
     We are God's people, sheep of the flock.

4   Enter the gates with thanksgiving,
     God's courts with songs of praise.
     Give thanks to God and bless his name.

5   Indeed, how good is the Lord,
     whose merciful love is eternal;
     whose faithfulness lasts forever.

---

*The seventh step of humility is that a man
is also convinced in his heart that he is
inferior to all and of less value.*

(126) 127. Praise of God's Goodness: A Pilgrimage Song

1   If the Lord does not build the house,
     in vain do its builders labor;
     if the Lord does not watch over the city,
     in vain do the watchers keep vigil.

2   In vain is your earlier rising,
     your going later to rest,
     you who toil for the bread you eat,
     when God pours gifts on the beloved while they slumber.

3   Yes, children are a gift from the Lord,
     a blessing, the fruit of the womb.
4   The sons and daughters of youth
     are like arrows in the hand of a warrior.

5   O the happiness of those
     who have filled their quiver with these arrows!
     They will have no cause for shame
     when they dispute with their foes in the gateways.

Evil speech be curbed so that punishment
for sin may be avoided.

(135) 136.   Litany of Praises: Psalm of Worship

1   Alleluia!
    O give thanks to the Lord who is good,
    whose love endures forever.
2   Give thanks to the God of gods,
    whose love endures forever.
3   Give thanks to the Lord of lords,
    whose love endures forever;

4   who alone has wrought marvelous works,
    whose love endures forever;
5   whose wisdom it was made the skies,
    whose love endures forever;
6   who fixed the earth firmly on the seas,
    whose love endures forever.

7   It was God who made the great lights,
    whose love endures forever;
8   the sun to rule in the day,
    whose love endures forever;
9   the moon and stars in the night,
    whose love endures forever.

Be discerning and moderate.

10	The first-born of the Egyptians God smote,
	whose love endures forever;
11	and brought Israel out from the midst,
	whose love endures forever;
12	arm outstretched, with powerful hand,
	whose love endures forever.

13	God divided the Red Sea in two,
	whose love endures forever;
14	and made Israel pass through the midst,
	whose love endures forever;
15	Who flung Pharaoh and his force in the sea,
	whose love endures forever.

16	God led the people through the desert,
	whose love endures forever.
17	Nations in their greatness God struck,
	whose love endures forever.
18	Kings in their splendor God slew,
	whose love endures forever.

19	Sihon, king of the Amorites,
	whose love endures forever;
20	and Og, the king of Bashan,
	whose love endures forever.

Place your hope in God alone.

21	God let Israel inherit their land,
	whose love endures forever;
22	the heritage of Israel, God's servant,
	whose love endures forever.
23	God remembered us in our distress,
	whose love endures forever.
24	God has snatched us away from our foes,
	whose love endures forever.
25	God gives food to all living things,
	whose love endures forever.
26	To the God of heaven give thanks,
	whose love endures forever.

Never give a hollow greeting of peace.

148. Cosmic Praise

1   Alleluia!

Praise the Lord from the heavens,
praise God in the heights.
2   Praise God, all you angels,
praise him, all you host.

3   Praise God, sun and moon,
praise him, shining stars.
4   Praise God, highest heavens
and the waters above the heavens.

5   Let them praise the name of the Lord.
The Lord commanded: they were made.
6   God fixed them forever,
gave a law which shall not pass away.

7   Praise the Lord from the earth,
sea creatures and all oceans,
8   fire and hail, snow and mist,
stormy winds that obey God's word;

9   all mountains and hills,
all fruit trees and cedars,
10 beasts, wild and tame,
reptiles and birds on the wing;

---

*He should not be prone to greed, nor be
wasteful and extravagant.*

11   all earth's nations and peoples,
      earth's leaders and rulers;
12   young men and maidens,
      the old together with children.

13   Let them praise the name of the Lord
      who alone is exalted.
      The splendor of God's name
      reaches beyond heaven and earth.

14   God exalts the strength of the people,
      is the praise of all the saints,
      of the sons and daughters of Israel,
      of the people to whom he comes close.

      Alleluia!

---

*Speaking and teaching are the master's
task; the disciple is to be silent and listen.*

149.   Praise to the God of Victories

1   Alleluia!

Sing a new song to the Lord,
Sing praise in the assembly of the faithful.
2   Let Israel rejoice in its Maker,
let Zion's people exult in their king.
3   Let them praise God's name with dancing
and make music with timbrel and harp.

4   For the Lord takes delight in his people,
and crowns the poor with salvation.
5   Let the faithful rejoice in their glory,
shout for joy and take their rest.
6   Let the praise of God be on their lips
and a two-edged sword in their hand,

7   to deal out vengeance to the nations
and punishment on all the peoples;
8   to bind their kings in chains
and their nobles in fetters of iron;
9   to carry out the sentence pre-ordained:
this honor is for all God's faithful.

Alleluia!

Do everything with moderation.

150. Praise the Lord

1   Alleluia!

Praise God in his holy place,
Sing praise in the mighty heavens.
2   Sing praise for God's powerful deeds,
praise God's surpassing greatness.

3   Sing praise with sound of trumpet,
Sing praise with lute and harp.
4   Sing praise with timbrel and dance,
Sing praise with strings and pipes.

5   Sing praise with resounding cymbals,
Sing praise with clashing of cymbals.
6   Let everything that lives and that breathes
give praise to the Lord. Alleluia!

---

*Never turn away when someone needs
your love.*

Magnificat—Luke 1:46-55

46   And Mary said, "My soul magnifies the Lord,
47   and my spirit rejoices in God my Savior,
48   for he has looked with favor on the
     lowliness of his servant.
     Surely, from now on all generations
     will call me blessed;
49   for the Mighty One has done great
     things for me, and holy is his name.
50   His mercy is for those who fear him
     from generation to generation.
51   He has shown strength with his arm;
     he has scattered the proud in
     the thoughts of their hearts.
52   He has brought down the powerful from
     their thrones, and lifted up the lowly;
53   he has filled the hungry with good things,
     and sent the rich away empty.
54   He has helped his servant Israel,
     in remembrance of his mercy,
55   according to the promise he made to
     our ancestors, to Abraham and to his
     descendants forever."

We are forbidden to do our own will.

Benedictus—Luke 1:68-79

68   "Blessed be the Lord God of Israel,
for he has looked favorably on
his people and redeemed them.

69   He has raised up a mighty savior
for us in the house of his servant David,

70   as he spoke through the mouth of
his holy prophets from of old,

71   that we would be saved from our enemies
and from the hand of all who hate us.

72   Thus he has shown the mercy
promised to our ancestors, and has
remembered his holy covenant,

73   the oath that he swore to our
ancestor Abraham, to grant us

74   that we, being rescued from the hands of
our enemies, might serve him without fear,

75   in holiness and righteousness
before him all our days.

76   And you, child, will be called the
prophet of the Most High: for you will
go before the Lord to prepare his ways,

77   to give knowledge of salvation to his
people by the forgiveness of their sins.

78   By the tender mercy of our God, the
dawn from on high will break upon us,

79   to give light to those who sit in
darkness and in the shadow of death,
to guide our feet into the way of peace."

Let him keep watch over his own soul.

Nunc Dimittis—Luke 2:29-32

29   "Master, now you are dismissing
       your servant in peace,
       according to your word;
30   for my eyes have seen your salvation,
31   which you have prepared in the
       presence of all peoples,
32   a light for revelation to the Gentiles
       and for glory to your people Israel."

---

*Those to whom God gives the strength to
abstain must know that they will earn
their own reward.*

Philippians 2:5-11

5   Let the same mind be in you
that was in Christ Jesus,
6   who, though he was
in the form of God,
did not regard equality with God
as something to be exploited,
7   but emptied himself,
taking the form of a slave,
being born in human likeness.
And being found in human form,
8   he humbled himself and became
obedient to the point of death—
even death on a cross.

9   Therefore God also highly exalted him
and gave him the name
that is above every name,
10   so that at the name of Jesus
every knee should bend,
in heaven and on earth
and under the earth,
11   and every tongue should confess
that Jesus Christ is Lord,
to the glory of God the Father.

Let all the rest serve one another in love.

GENERAL
PRAYERS

Our Father

Our Father, who art in heaven,
hallowed be thy name;
thy kingdom come;
thy will be done on earth as it is in heaven.
Give us this day our daily bread;
and forgive us our trespasses
as we forgive those who trespass against us;
and lead us not into temptation,
but deliver us from evil.

For thine is the kingdom, the power and the glory now
and forever.

Amen.

Deliver us, Lord, from every evil,
and grant us peace in our day.
In your mercy,
keep us free from sin,
and protect us from all anxiety
as we wait in joyful hope
for the coming of Our Savior Jesus Christ.

To do battle for the true King,
Christ the Lord.

The Apostles Creed

I believe in God the Father almighty,
creator of heaven and earth;
and in Jesus Christ, His only Son, our Lord,
who was conceived by the Holy Spirit,
born of the Virgin Mary,
suffered under Pontius Pilate,
was crucified, died, and was buried.
He descended into hell;
the third day he rose again from the dead.
He ascended into heaven,
and is seated at the right hand of the Father
from where he shall come to judge the
living and the dead.

I believe in the Holy Spirit,
the Holy Catholic Church,
the Communion of Saints,
the forgiveness of sins,
the resurrection of the body,
and life everlasting.

Amen.

---

*The life of a monk ought to be a
continuous Lent.*

Doxology (Saint Meinrad Translation)

Glory to the Father, and the Son,
and the Holy Spirit;
as always before,
so now, and evermore.

Amen.

Doxology (Traditional English Translation)

Glory be to the Father, and to the Son,
and to the Holy Spirit;
as it was in the beginning, is now,
and ever shall be, world without end.

Amen.

---

*Refrain from too much eating or sleeping,
and from laziness.*

Prayer Before Meals

Bless us, O Lord, and these, your gifts,
which we are about to receive from your bounty,
through Christ, our Lord.

Amen.

Prayer After Meals

We give you thanks, O God,
for these and all your benefits,
through Christ, our Lord.

Amen.

---

*If people curse you, do not curse them back
but bless them instead.*

Come, Holy Spirit

V. Come, Holy Spirit.
R. Fill the hearts of your faithful
and enkindle within them the fire of your love.

V. Send forth your Spirit and they shall be created.
R. And you shall renew the face of the earth.

Let us pray:

O God,
you have instructed the hearts of the faithful
by the light of the Holy Spirit.
Grant that through the same Holy Spirit
we may always be truly wise
and rejoice in his consolation.
Through Christ our Lord.

Amen.

He may simply go in and pray, not in a
loud voice, but with tears and
heartfelt devotion.

Divine Praises

Blessed be God.
Blessed be his Holy Name.
Blessed be Jesus Christ, true God and true Man.
Blessed be the Name of Jesus.
Blessed be his most Sacred Heart.
Blessed be his most Precious Blood.
Blessed be Jesus in the most holy Sacrament of the Altar.
Blessed be the Holy Spirit, the Paraclete.
Blessed be the great Mother of God, Mary most holy.
Blessed be her holy and Immaculate Conception.
Blessed be her glorious Assumption.
Blessed be the name of Mary, virgin and mother.
Blessed be St. Joseph, her most chaste spouse.
Blessed be God in his angels and in his saints.

Proper honor must be shown to all.

Praises of God

You are holy, Lord, the only God,
and your deeds are wonderful.
You are strong.
You are great.
You are the Most High,
You are almighty.
You, holy Father, are
King of heaven and earth.
You are Three and One,
Lord God, all good.
You are good, all good, supreme good,
Lord God, living and true.
You are love,
You are wisdom
You are humility,
You are endurance
You are rest,
You are peace.
You are joy and gladness.
You are justice and moderation.
You are all our riches,
and you suffice for us.
You are beauty.
You are gentleness.
You are our protector,
You are our guardian and defender.
You are courage.

Do not pamper yourself, but love fasting.

You are our haven and our hope.
You are our faith,
our great consolation.
You are our eternal life,
great and wonderful Lord,
God almighty, merciful Savior.

St. Francis of Assisi

---

*If you notice something good in yourself,
give credit to God, not to yourself.*

The Beatitudes

Blessed are the poor in spirit, for theirs is the kingdom of heaven.

Blessed are those who mourn, for they will be comforted.

Blessed are the meek, for they will inherit the earth.

Blessed are those who hunger and thirst for righteousness, for they will be filled.

Blessed are the merciful, for they will receive mercy.

Blessed are the pure in heart, for they will see God.

Blessed are the peacemakers, for they will be called children of God.

Blessed are those who are persecuted for righteousness' sake, for theirs is the kingdom of heaven.

Blessed are you when people revile you and persecute you and utter all kinds of evil against you falsely on my account. Rejoice and be glad, for your reward is great in heaven, for in the same way they persecuted the prophets who were before you.

Matthew 5:3-11

Make more and more progress toward God.

Act of Faith

O my God,
I firmly believe that You are one God
in three Divine Persons,
the Father, Son and Holy Spirit.
I believe that Your Divine Son
became man and died for our sins,
and that He will come to judge
the living and the dead.
I believe these and all the truths,
which the Holy Catholic Church teaches,
because You have revealed them,
Who can neither deceive nor be deceived.

Act of Hope

O my God,
relying on Your infinite goodness and promises,
I hope to obtain pardon for my sins,
the help of Your grace,
and life everlasting,
through the merits of Jesus Christ,
my Lord and Redeemer.

Amen.

Do not injure anyone.

Act of Love

O my God,
I love You above all things,
with my whole heart and soul,
because You are all good and worthy of all my love.
I love my neighbor as myself
for the love of You.
I forgive all who have injured me
and ask pardon for all whom I have injured.

Amen.

---

*Our hearts overflowing with the
inexpressible delight of love.*

Anima Christi

Soul of Christ, sanctify me;
Body of Christ, save me.
Blood of Christ, inebriate me;
water from the side of Christ, wash me.
Passion of Christ, strengthen me.
O Good Jesus, hear me.
Never permit me to be separated from you.
From the evil one protect me,
at the hour of death call me,
and bid me to come to you
that with your saints I may
praise you forever.

Amen.

Bear injuries patiently.

The Sufferer's Prayer

As daily at the altar prays the priest
and elevates the host above his head
so offer I my body on this bed,
my frail and broken body, fever-burnt;
in hours of pain this lesson have I learnt:
I join myself with Jesus on His cross
so nothing of my pain is ever lost.
This is my body, Christ, lift it on high;
receive each muffled groan and every sigh,
for suffering borne helps me keep afresh
the likeness of Our Savior in my flesh.

Walter Sullivan, OSB

Be learned in divine law.

Prayer for One Near Death

Go forth, Christian soul, from this world
in the name of God the almighty Father,
who created you,
in the name of Jesus Christ, Son of the living God,
who suffered for you,
in the name of the Holy Spirit,
who has poured out upon you,
go forth, good Christian.
May you live in peace this day,
may your home be with God in Zion,
with Mary, the Virgin Mother of God,
with Joseph, and all the angels and saints.

Saints of God, come to his/her aid!
Come to greet him/her, angels of the Lord!

From: *Pastoral Care of the Sick: Rites of Anointing and Viaticum*

Diligently cultivate silence at all times,
but especially at night.

Prayer for One Who Has Died

Holy Lord, almighty and eternal God,
hear our prayers for your servant N.,
whom you have summoned out of this world.
Forgive his/her sins and failings
and grant him/her a place of refreshment, light and peace.
Let him/her pass unharmed through the gates of death
to dwell with the blessed in light,
as you promised to Abraham and his children for ever.
Accept N. into your safekeeping
and on the great day of judgment
raise him/her up with all the saints
to inherit your eternal kingdom.

We ask this through Christ our Lord.

Amen.

From: *The Order of Christian Funerals*

---

*We must then be on guard against any
base desire.*

Prayer for Mourners

Father of mercies and God of all consolation,
you pursue us with untiring love
and dispel the shadow of death
with the bright dawn of life.

Comfort your family in their loss and sorrow.
Be our refuge and our strength, O Lord,
and lift us from the depths of grief
into the peace and light of your presence.

Your Son, our Lord Jesus Christ,
by dying has destroyed our death,
and by rising, restored our life.
Enable us therefore to press on toward him,
so that, after our earthly course is run,
he may reunite us with those we love,
when every tear will be wiped away.

We ask this through Christ our Lord.

Amen.

From: *The Order of Christian Funerals*

*Those to whom God gives the strength to
abstain must know that they will earn
their own reward.*

And Peace at Last

May the Lord support us
all the day long
till the shadows lengthen
and the evening comes,
and the busy world is hushed,
and the fever of life is o'er,
and our work is done!
Then in his mercy
may he give us a safe lodging,
and a holy rest,
and peace at the last!

Cardinal Newman

*Human nature itself is inclined to be
compassionate toward the old
and the young.*

Prayer of Abandonment

Father,
I abandon myself into Your hands;
do with me what You will.
Whatever You may do, I thank you.

I am ready for all, I accept all.
Let only Your will be done in me,
and in all Your creatures
I wish no more than this, O Lord.

Into Your hands I commend my soul;
I offer it to You
with all the love of my heart,
for I love You, Lord,
and so,
I need to give myself,
to surrender myself,
into Your hands
without reserve
and with boundless confidence,
for You are my Father.

Br. Charles of Jesus

*They are to pray together and thus be
united in peace.*

Prayer for Serenity

God, grant me serenity
to accept the things I cannot change,
courage to change the things I can
and wisdom to know the difference.
Living one day at a time,
enjoying one moment at a time,
accepting hardship as a pathway to peace,
taking, as Jesus did,
this sinful world as it is,
not as I would have it,
trusting that You will make all things right
if I surrender to Your will,
so that I may be reasonably happy in this life
and supremely happy with You forever in the next.

Amen.

Reinhold Niebuhr

---

*In truth, those who are patient amid
hardships and unjust treatment are
fulfilling the Lord's command.*

Prayer in Honor of St. Benedict

Raise up in your Church, O Lord,
that spirit which animated St. Benedict,
that filled with that same spirit,
we may learn to love what he loved
and to practice what he taught.
Through Christ our Lord.

Amen.

---

*Our hearts overflowing with the
inexpressible delight of love.*

Prayer in Honor of St. Meinrad

O God, you are made glorious in the
martyrdom of the hermit Meinrad.
Through his intercession
help me to grow in my love for you
and in devotion to the Blessed Virgin Mary.
May I follow his example
in Christ-like hospitality
and in single hearted prayer.
Through Christ our Lord.

Amen.

*Be certain that the evil you commit is
always your own and yours to acknowledge.*

Prayer in Honor of St. Scholastica

Almighty God,
in your goodness you called the virgin Scholastica
to embrace the monastic life of her brother, Benedict.
Through her prayers,
help me to hear your call in my life and,
at my death,
grant that I might praise you forever in heaven.
Through Christ our Lord.

Amen.

Be on guard against conceit or pride.

The Prayer of St. Francis

Lord, make me an instrument of your peace.

Where there is hatred, let me sow love
Where there is injury, pardon
Where there is doubt, faith
Where there is despair, hope
Where there is darkness, light
Where there is sadness, joy.

O Divine Master,
Grant that I may not so much seek
to be consoled as to console
to be understood as to understand
to be loved as to love.

For it is in giving that we receive
it is in pardoning that we are pardoned
it is in dying that we are born to eternal life.

Yearn for everlasting life with holy desire.

St. Patrick's Breastplate

I bind unto myself today
the strong name of the Trinity,
by invocation of the same,
The Three in One,
and One in Three.

I bind this day to me forever,
by power of faith,
Christ's incarnation;
His baptism in Jordan river;
His death on the cross for my salvation;
His bursting from the spiced tomb;
His riding up the heavenly way;
His coming at the day of doom;
I bind unto myself today.

I bind unto myself
the power of the great love of the Cherubim;
the sweet "well done" in judgement hour;
the service of the Seraphim,
confessors' faith, Apostles' word,
the patriarchs' prayers, the prophets' scrolls,
all good deeds done unto the Lord,
and purity of virgin souls.

Use prudence and avoid extremes.

I bind unto myself today
the virtues of the star-lit heaven,
the glorious sun's life-giving ray,
the whiteness of the moon at even,
the flashing of the lightning free,
the whirling wind's tempestuous shocks,
the stable earth, the deep salt sea,
around the old eternal rocks.

I bind unto myself today
the power of God to hold and lead,
His eye to watch, His might to stay,
His ear to harken to my need,
The wisdom of my God to teach,
His hand to guide, His shield to ward;
the word of God to give me speech,
His heavenly host to be my guard.

Against the demon snares of sin,
the vice that gives temptation force,
the natural lusts that war within,
the hostile men that mar my course;
or few or many, far or nigh,
in every place, and in all hours,
against their fierce hostility,
I bind to me these holy powers.

---

*He is to distrust his own frailty and
remember not to crush the bruised reed.*

Against all Satan's spells and wiles,
against false words of heresy,
against the knowledge that defiles,
against the heart's idolatry,
against the wizard's evil craft,
against the death-wound and the burning,
the choking wave, the poisoned shaft,
protect me, Christ, till thy returning.

Christ be with me, Christ within me,
Christ behind me, Christ before me,
Christ beside me, Christ to win me,
Christ to comfort and restore me,
Christ beneath me, Christ above me,
Christ in quiet, Christ in danger,
Christ in hearts of all that love me,
Christ in mouth of friend and stranger.

I bind unto myself the name,
the strong name of the Trinity;
by invocation of the same,
the Three in One, and One in Three.

Of whom all nature hath creation;
eternal Father, Spirit, Word:
praise to the Lord of my salvation,
salvation is of Christ the Lord.

Amen.

Hour by hour keep careful watch
over all you do.

The Road Ahead

My Lord God
I have no idea where I am going.
I do not see the road ahead of me.
I cannot know for certain where it will end.
Nor do I really know myself,
and the fact that I think I am following your will
does not mean that I am actually doing so.
But I believe that the desire to please you
does in fact please you.
And I hope that I have that desire
in all that I am doing.
I hope that I will never do anything
apart from that desire.
And I know that if I do this,
you will lead me by the right road,
though I may know nothing about it.
Therefore I will trust you always,
though I may seem to be lost
and in the shadow of death.
I will not fear,
for you are ever with me
and you will never leave me to face my perils alone.

Fr. Thomas Merton, OCSO

*Day by day remind yourself that you are
going to die.*

JESUS
IN·MY·HEART
I·BELIEVE
IN·YOUR
TENDER·LOVE
FOR·ME
I·LOVE
YOU

MOTHER TERESA

Adoro te devote

Adoro te devote, latens Deitas,
Quae sub his figuris vere latitas:
Tibi se cor meum totum subiicit,
Quia te contemplans totum deficit.

Visus, tactus, gustus in te fallitur,
Sed auditu solo tuto creditur.
Credo, quidquid dixit Dei Filius:
Nil hoc verbo Veritatis verius.

In cruce latebat sola Deitas,
At hic latet simul et humanitas;
Ambo tamen credens atque confitens,
Peto quod petivit latro paenitans.

Plagas, sicut Thomas, non intueor;
Deum tamen meum te confiteor.
Fac me tibi semper magis credere,
In te spem habere, te dilgere.

O memoriale mortis Domini!
Panis vivus, vitam praestans hoimini!
Praseta meae menti de te vivere.
Et te illi semper dulce sapere.

Pie pellicane, Iesu Domine,
Me immundum munda tuo sanguine.
Cuius una stilla salvum facere
Totum mundum quit ab omni scelere.

Iesu, quem velatum nunc aspicio,
Oro fiat illud quod tam sitio;
Ut te revelata cernens facie,
Visu sim beatus tuae gloriae.

Amen.

---

*Let him strive to be loved rather
than feared.*

Adoro te devote

I devoutly adore You, O hidden God
truly hidden beneath these appearances.
My whole heart submits to You
and in contemplating You
it surrenders itself completely.

Sight, touch, taste are all deceived
in their judgment of You,
but hearing suffices firmly to believe.
I believe all that the Son of God has spoken:
there is nothing truer than this word of Truth.

On the Cross only the Divinity was hidden,
but here the Humanity is also hidden.
I believe and confess both
and I ask for what the repentant thief asked.

I do not see the wounds as Thomas did,
but I confess that You are my God.
Make me believe more and more in You,
hope in You, and love You.

O Memorial of our Lord's death!
Living Bread that gives life to man,
grant my soul to live on in You
and always to savor Your sweetness.

Lord Jesus, good Pelican,
wash me clean with Your Blood,
one drop of which can free
the entire world of all its sins.

Jesus, whom now I see hidden,
I ask You to fulfill what I so desire:
that on seeing You face to face,
I may be happy in seeing Your glory. Amen.

Arrange everything that the strong have
something to yearn for and the weak
nothing to run from.

Father, You created me
to be Your living temple.
I open myself to Your
presence. Come and live
in me. May Your Holy
Spirit, living and work=
ing in me, transform
me into the likeness of
Your beloved Son, Jesus.

THE WAY OF
THE CROSS

The Way of the Cross

A pilgrimage to the Holy Land has always been the desire of many of the faithful. Unfortunately, most people are not able to fulfill that desire. The "Stations of the Cross" arose as a way of allowing those unable to go to the Holy Places the opportunity of sharing in the grace of such a trip.

In Jerusalem, it was the custom to walk through the city on what was called the "way of sorrow." This "way" was eventually standardized. This walk on the "way of sorrow" was realized in parish churches by the erection of wooden crosses, or stations where the faithful could walk and pray. The erection of these stations had required the approval of the Franciscans, who were in charge of the shrines in Jerusalem.

Gradually, pictorial images of the fourteen stations began to appear. Still, as now, the small wooden crosses constitute the actual stations.

The Traditional Stations of the Cross:

1.   Jesus is condemned by Pilate

2.   Jesus takes up his cross

3.   Jesus falls the first time

4.   Jesus meets his mother

5.   Simon of Cyrene helps Jesus carry his cross

6.   Veronica wipes the face of Jesus

---

*As soon as wrongful thoughts come into
your heart, dash them against Christ.*

7.   Jesus falls the second time

8.   Jesus meets the women of Jerusalem

9.   Jesus falls the third time

10.   Jesus is stripped

11.   Jesus is nailed to the cross

12.   Jesus dies on the cross

13.   Jesus is taken down from the cross

14.   Jesus is buried

Several of the traditional fourteen stations are based on legend rather than the Gospel accounts of the passion. In 1991, Pope John Paul II began using a revised set of stations that are based on the Scriptures.

The Revised Stations of the Cross (Pope John Paul II):

1.   Jesus in the Garden of Olives

2.   Jesus is betrayed by Judas and arrested

3.   Jesus is condemned by the Sanhedrin

4.   Jesus is denied by Peter

5.   Jesus is condemned by Pilate

6.   Jesus is scourged and crowned with thorns

7.   Jesus is made to carry his cross

Respect the elders and love the young.

8.   Simon of Cyrene helps Jesus carry his cross

9.   Jesus meets the women of Jerusalem

10.   Jesus is crucified

11.   Jesus promises the Kingdom to the repentant thief

12.   Jesus speaks to his mother and to the beloved disciple

13.   Jesus dies on the cross

14.   Jesus is laid in the tomb

After the meditation on each station in both sets, the following is prayed:

V. We adore you, O Christ, and we bless you.

R. Because by your holy cross you have
redeemed the world.

---

*Guard your lips from harmful or
deceptive speech.*

MARIAN
PRAYERS

Hail Mary

Hail Mary, full of grace,
the Lord is with thee.
Blessed art thou amongst women,
and blessed is the fruit of thy womb, Jesus.
Holy Mary, Mother of God,
pray for us sinners,
now and at the hour of our death.

Amen.

By this way of obedience we go to God.

The Angelus

V. The Angel of the Lord declared unto Mary...
R. and she conceived of the Holy Spirit.

Hail Mary...

V. Behold the handmaid of the Lord...
R. be it done to me according to thy word.

Hail Mary...

V. The Word became flesh...
R. and dwelt among us.

Hail Mary...

Let us pray:

Pour forth, we beseech thee,
your grace into our hearts,
that we to whom the incarnation of Christ your Son,
was made known through the message of an angel,
might through his passion and cross
be brought to the glory of the resurrection.
Through the same Christ our Lord.

Amen.

*The eighth step of humility is that a monk
does only what is endorsed by the common
rule of the monastery.*

Hail, Holy Queen

Hail, holy queen,
mother of mercy,
our life, our sweetness and our hope.
To you do we cry,
poor banished children of Eve.
To you do we send up our sighs,
mourning and weeping in this valley of tears.
Turn then, most gracious advocate,
thine eyes of mercy toward us,
and after this our exile,
show us the blessed fruit of thy womb, Jesus.
O kind, O loving, O sweet Virgin Mary.

Do not grumble or speak ill of others.

Memorare

Remember, O most gracious Virgin Mary,
that never was it known
that anyone who fled to thy protection,
implored thy help,
or sought thy intercession, was left unaided.
Inspired by this confidence,
I fly unto thee, O Virgin of virgins, my Mother.
To thee I come, before thee I stand,
sinful and sorrowful.
O Mother of the Word Incarnate,
despise not my petitions,
but in thy mercy hear and answer me.

Amen.

Live by God's commandments every day.

Antiphon of Our Lady of Einsiedeln

V. I am very dark, but lovely, O daughters of Jerusalem.
R. Therefore the king has loved me
and brought me into his chambers.

Lady of Einsiedeln, pray for us.

O God, you have blessed us with the loving
protection of the Blessed Virgin Mary.
Through the intercession of Our Lady of Einsieldeln,
hear our prayers and keep us in your constant care.
Through Christ our Lord.

Amen.

---

*The ninth step of humility is that a monk
controls his tongue and remains silent, not
speaking unless asked a question.*

Pilgrim Prayer to Our Lady of Monte Cassino

Dearest Mother Mary,
attracted to you by your goodness,
sympathy, and motherliness,
and also because of our needs,
we have come as pilgrims to your shrine today.

We love you, dearest Mother,
and we pray that we may learn
to love you more and more.
We ask you to keep us always
under your special protection,
and to help us in all of our needs.
Please listen with love
to the prayers and petitions of
all who come to this shrine
to seek your aid and to honor you.

Also, obtain for each one of us
through your powerful intercession
with Jesus, your Son,
all the graces we need to lead good lives
and follow his teachings,
especially his command to love one another.

Amen.

We shall through patience share in the
sufferings of Christ that we may deserve
also to share in his kingdom.

ALMA REDEMPTORIS

V A̱l- ma * Red-emp-to-ris Ma-ter, quae per-vi-a cae-li Por-

ta ma-nes, et stel-la ma-ris, suc-cur-re ca-den-ti, Sur-ge-re qui

cu-rat, po-pu-lo: Tu quae ge-nu-is-ti, Na-tu-ra mi-ran-te, tu-um

sanc-tum Ge-ni-to-rem, Vir-go pri-us, ac pos-te-ri-us, Gab-ri-e-

lis ab o-re Su-mens il-lud A-ve, pec-ca-to-rum mi-se-re-re.

AVE REGINA

VI

A — VE Re- gi-na cae-lo-rum, * Ave Domi-na Ange-

lo-rum Salve ra-dix, salve porta, Ex qua mundo lux

est orta: Gaude Virgo glo- ri- o- sa, Su- per omnes spe-

ci- o-sa: Va-le O valde de- co-ra, Et pro no- bis Christum

ex- o- ra.

REGINA COELI

VI

℟ E - gi-na coe-li *lae-ta-re, al-le-lu-ia:

Qui-a quem me-ru-i-sti portare, al-le-lu-ia:

Re-sur-re-xit, sic-ut di-xit, al-le-lu-ia:

O- ra pro no- bis De-um, al-le- lu-ia.

SALVE REGINA

SALVE Regi- na, * ma-ter mi- e-ri-cor- di-ae, Vi-ta, dul-

ce-do, et spes nostra, salve. Ad te clamamus, exsules, fi-li-i

Hevae. Ad te suspi-ramus, gementes et flentes in hac lacri-

marum valle. E-ia ergo, Advo-ca-ta nostra, il-los tu-os mi-

se-ri-cordes o-cu-los ad nos conver-te. Et Je-sum, be-ne-

dictum fructum ventris tu-i, no-bis post hoc ex- si- li- um o-

stende. O cle-mens, O pi-a, O dulcis * Virgo Mari-a.

BEHOLD,
I AM THE

Handmaid
of the Lord

LET IT BE TO ME
ACCORDING TO YOUR WILL.

LUKE 1:38

The Rosary

The rosary has its origin in the monasteries of Europe. St. Benedict desired that the monks pray all 150 psalms over the course of a week. In order to allow those monks who worked the fields to participate in the community's prayer, they substituted 150 "Our Fathers" for the 150 psalms. This quickly became popular among ordinary men and women. The "Paters," as they were called, were counted on a string of 150 beads.

Eventually, the "Our Fathers" were replaced with "Hail Marys." As it grew in popularity, the rosary lost its original connection to the Liturgy of the Hours and became a means of personal devotion. Because of the Gospel injunction to avoid the mere repetition of words, people were encouraged to use the rosary as a means of meditating on the life of the Lord Jesus and his mother. Gradually, specific sets of mysteries became attached to decades of the rosary.

The Dominican Order was quite influential in spreading the use of the rosary. It was from this historical reality that the legend of St. Dominic receiving the rosary from the Blessed Virgin Mary arose. There is no historical basis for this legend.

The rosary is primarily a personal prayer. Group recitation of the rosary has been popular in various times and places, but is not really in keeping with the rosary's evolution into a tool for meditation.

If you have a dispute with someone, make peace with him before the sun goes down.

The rosary is a venerable part of the Catholic tradition of prayer, but it is not for everyone. As Pope Paul VI wrote in his Encyclical on Mary, "The faithful should feel completely free in this regard."

When people today speak of praying the rosary, they are usually referring to five decades. Most rosaries, in fact, are made with five decades of beads. These five decades focus on a particular set of mysteries. These mysteries are meditated on during the quiet praying of the appropriate prayers.

The faithful should feel free to meditate on any mystery of the life of Christ and his Blessed Mother.

Mysteries of the Rosary

Joyful Mysteries (Monday and Saturday)

1. The Annunciation

2. The Visitation

3. The Nativity

4. The Presentation

5. The Finding of the Child Jesus in the Temple

Sorrowful Mysteries (Tuesday and Friday)

1. The Agony in the Garden

2. The Scourging at the Pillar

The tenth step of humility is that he is not given to ready laughter.

3. The Crowning with Thorns

4. The Carrying of the Cross

5. The Crucifixion and Death of our Lord

Glorious Mysteries (Wednesday and Sunday)

1. The Resurrection

2. The Ascension

3. The Descent of the Holy Spirit

4. The Assumption

5. The Coronation of the Blessed Virgin

Luminous Mysteries (Thursday)

1. The Baptism in the Jordan

2. The Wedding at Cana

3. The Proclamation of the Kingdom

4. The Transfiguration

5. The Institution of the Eucharist

Be aware that God's gaze is upon you,
wherever you may be.

Praying the Rosary

At the crucifix: The Sign of the Cross and the Apostles Creed.

At the first bead: Our Father.

At the next three beads: Hail Mary.

At the first bead after the medal: The first mystery and Our Father.

At the next ten beads: ten Hail Marys followed by the Doxology.

This pattern continues through the next four decades, each beginning with the appropriate mystery.

At the medal: Hail Holy Queen.

At the crucifix: The sign of the Cross.

Prayer after the Rosary

Gracious, Loving Father, you gave us eternal life through the life, death and resurrection of your beloved Son, Jesus. Help us to meditate on these mysteries in the holy rosary of the most holy virgin, Mary, our Mother, so that we may imitate what they contain and obtain what they promise.

Obedience is a blessing to be shown by all.

ONGOING
CONVERSION
and
THE SACRAMENT
OF RECONCILIATION

Twelve Steps of Alcoholics Anonymous

(see disclaimer on page v of Acknowledgements)

How it Works

Rarely have we seen a person fail who has thoroughly followed our path. Those who do not recover are people who cannot or will not completely give themselves to this simple program, usually men and women who are constitutionally incapable of being honest with themselves. There are such unfortunates. They are not at fault; they seem to have been born that way. They are naturally incapable of grasping and developing a manner of living which demands rigorous honesty. Their chances are less than average. There are those, too, who suffer from grave emotional and mental disorders, but many of them do recover if they have the capacity to be honest.

Our stories disclose in a general way what we used to be like, what happened, and what we are like now. If you have decided you want what we have and are willing to go to any length to get it—then you are ready to take certain steps.

At some of these we balked. We thought we could find an easier, softer way. But we could not. With all the earnestness at our command, we beg of you to be fearless and thorough from the very start. Some of us have tried to hold on to our old ideas and the result was nil until we let go absolutely.

---

*It is love that impels them to pursue
everlasting life.*

Remember that we deal with alcohol—cunning, baffling, powerful! Without help it is too much for us. But there is One who has all power—that One is God. May you find Him now!

Half measures availed us nothing. We stood at the turning point. We asked His protection and care with complete abandon.

Here are the steps we took, which are suggested as a program of recovery:

1. We admitted we were powerless over alcohol, that our lives had become unmanageable.
2. Came to believe that a Power greater than ourselves could restore us to sanity.
3. Made a decision to turn our will and our lives over to the care of God *as we understood Him.*
4. Made a searching and fearless moral inventory of ourselves.
5. Admitted to God, to ourselves, and to another human being the exact nature of our wrongs.
6. Were entirely ready to have God remove all these defects of character.
7. Humbly asked Him to remove our shortcomings.
8. Made a list of all persons we had harmed, and became willing to make amends to them all.
9. Made direct amends to such people wherever possible, except when to do so would injure them or others.

Pray for your enemies out of love
for Christ.

10. Continued to take personal inventory and when we were wrong promptly admitted it.
11. Sought through prayer and meditation to improve our conscious contact with God *as we understood Him*, praying only for knowledge of His will for us and the power to carry that out.
12. Having had a spiritual awakening as the result of these steps, we tried to carry this message to alcoholics, and to practice these principles in all our affairs.

Many of us exclaimed, "What an order! I can't go through with it." Do not be discouraged. No one among us has been able to maintain anything like perfect adherence to these principles. We are not saints. The point is, that we are willing to grow along spiritual lines. The principles we have set down are guides to progress. We claim spiritual progress rather than spiritual perfection.

Our description of the alcoholic, the chapter to the agnostic, and our personal adventures before and after make clear three pertinent ideas:

(a) That we were alcoholic and could not manage our own lives.

(b) That probably no human power could have relieved our alcoholism.

(c) That God could and would if He were sought.

Prefer moderation in speech.

Conducting an Examination of Conscience

The life and writings of St. Benedict offer a wealth of material for use in examining one's conscience, perhaps when reviewing the day's events before bed, in preparing for the sacrament of Reconciliation, or when making a personal inventory of one's life as part of the ongoing conversion of life.

Benedict of Nursia was born circa 480 A.D. As the son of a Roman nobleman, Benedict was raised in a home of abundant privilege and opportunity. Yet, as a young man, Benedict chose to leave Rome and the path of privilege and power that awaited him. St. Gregory wrote, "[Benedict] was in the world and was free to enjoy the advantages which the world offers, but drew back his foot which he had, as it were, already set forth in the world." (*New Advent*)

Benedict longed to serve God and, to that end, he settled 40 miles outside Rome, where he lived as a hermit for three years in the hills near Subiaco. Despite his isolated living situation, Benedict soon became known and respected by the people of the area, many of whom also experienced the same thirst for God that prompted Benedict to leave Rome.

We must know that God regards our
purity of heart and tears of compunction,
not our many words.

In response, Benedict founded 12 monastic communities, which eventually multiplied throughout Europe. Then, as now, Benedictine and Cistercian monastic communities (and their oblates) live under the *Rule of St. Benedict*, which guides their life together.

The *Rule of St. Benedict*

Though the *Rule* was originally written for monastic communities, its value as a guide for the journey of Christian discipleship is widely recognized. Author Norveen Vest observed, "The whole orientation of the *Rule* is to the principle that God is everywhere, all the time, and thus that every element of our ordinary day is potentially holy…. Because the *Rule* is so 'homely,' so oriented to the opportunities of daily life as grist for the mill of Christian consecration, it has a great deal to say which is directly helpful to a Christian lay person, struggling to live the Christian life even in our contemporary secular world." (*Oblate Formation Booklet*)

Still, the principles and values highlighted in the *Rule* are not intended to be rungs on a ladder reaching toward God, but milestones along the journey of faith. For as Benedictine monk Michael Casey noted, "St. Benedict has a very high estimation of the importance of grace in spiritual life." Therefore, "to picture [spiritual] life as a process of exaltation clearly emphasizes that it is God who is the

---

Speak no foolish chatter.

active agent; the [disciple] is the one who is lifted up" (*Casey, pp. 56-57*). Thus, the spiritual journey is less about the work we do to reach God, than creating space in our lives for God to reach us.

The *Rule* can serve as a touchstone for reflecting on your own journey of faith as you prepare to participate in the sacrament of Reconciliation. The 10 Benedictine values that are highlighted in the pages that follow will serve to guide you as you examine your relationship with God, others and the world.

Conversatio morum suorum - **Conversion of Life**

Listen readily to holy reading, and devote yourself often to prayer. Every day with tears and sighs confess your past sins to God in prayer and change from these evil ways in the future. Chapter 4:55-58 (RB 1980: The Rule of St. Benedict in English)

Listen, pray, confess your past sins, change for the future.
- How do you spend your time?
- How often do you create time for solitude and prayer?
- Is your prayer mostly talking or listening?
- What are the things you struggle with, the stumbling blocks that repeatedly cause you to trip?
- What do you want most to change about yourself? What steps are you taking to effect those changes? Who have

---

Prayer should therefore be short and pure, unless perhaps it is prolonged under the inspiration of divine grace.

you enlisted to assist you? To whom have you made yourself accountable?

Conversatio...*generally means a conversion of manners, a continuing and unsparing assessment and reassessment of one's self and what is valuable in life. In essence, the individual must continually ask, "What is worth living for in this place and time?"...Conversatio's objective was that each person become the self-constituting, good, holy, responsible person God intended him or her to be—to make their "city," wherever it might be, work.* (Paul Wilkes, p. 45)

What is worth living for?
• What are you willing to die for?
• What are you passionate about? What are you willing to do to follow your passion?

Become the person God intended you to be.
• What are the gifts and talents that God has given you? What are you doing to cultivate them? Where and how are you using your gifts?

Make your "city" work, wherever it might be.
• What are the contributions you make to your family, workplace, congregation, neighborhood, the world? How would these communities be different were you not part of them?

Never give a hollow greeting of peace.

Humility

Now, therefore, after ascending all these steps of humility, the monk will quickly arrive at the "perfect love" of God which "casts out fear" (1 John 4:18). *Through this love, all that he once performed with dread, he will now begin to observe without effort, as though naturally, from habit, no longer out of fear of hell, but out of love for Christ, good habit and delight in virtue. All this the Lord will by the Holy Spirit graciously manifest in his workman now cleansed of vices and sins.* Chapter 7:67-70 (RB 1980: The Rule of St. Benedict in English)

No longer out of fear of hell, but out of love for Christ.
• Feeling fearful is part of being human. What frightens you? How do you cope with fear?
• Who, and in what, do you trust?
• What gives you hope?
• What motivates your prayer, your life at home, at work and in your community?
• What are the images of God; how do they shape your thoughts and actions?

Humility is *"the capacity for receiving grace...a fundamental stance before God: a willingness to be saved, an openness to God's action, an assent to the mysterious processes by which God's plan is realized in the hearts of human beings... it is a receptivity or passivity; a matter of being acted upon by God."* (Columba Stewart, p. 56)

Care of the sick must rank above and before all else, so that they may truly be served as Christ.

Willingness to be saved
• What are your struggles, what is your "Achilles' heel"; in other words, from what do you need to be saved?
• To be saved implies that you need help. Are you willing to ask for help and to receive it?
• How do you respond when you receive a compliment, a gift or a favor? Do you feel restless until you reciprocate?

Openness to God's action
• How is God nudging you?
• Are you resisting? How?

Assent to the mysterious processes of God
• Acknowledge the boundaries of your "yes" to God. Map them. What are you willing and unwilling to do?
• In what aspects of your life are you willing to surrender to the experience of God?

Humility then is the foundation for our relationship with God, our connectedness to others, our acceptance of ourselves, our way of using the goods of the earth and even our way of walking through the world, without arrogance, without domination, without scorn, without put-downs, without disdain, without self-centeredness. The more we know ourselves, the gentler we will be with others. (Joan Chittister, The Rule of Benedict, p. 74)

Let him keep watch over his own soul.

Connectedness to others

• Examine the way in which you relate to others: family members, co-workers, neighbors, strangers, people to whom you are accountable as well as those who are accountable to you. Are you truthful and direct? Reliable? Trustworthy? Generous with your time, talents and material goods? Authentic?

• Are you able to see the Christ in others? What blocks your ability to see Christ in those around you?

Self-acceptance

• To whom do you feel a need to prove yourself?

• Where and with whom do you feel most accepted and valued?

Way of walking through the world

• Are there people you dismiss or look down upon, about whom you make assumptions? Acknowledge your prejudices.

• How do you relate to others? Do you feel the need to be right, to be in control? Are you more comfortable in the background? Do you speak up when necessary?

• Who do you struggle to accept and value? What steps are you willing to take to change this?

• Benedict tells us our way of acting should be different from the world's way. In what ways are you worldly? How should your way of acting change?

Proper honor must be shown to all.

Stability

When he is to be received, he comes before the whole community in the oratory and promises stability, fidelity to monastic life, and obedience. Chapter 58:17 (RB 1980: The Rule of St. Benedict in English)

Commitments
• What are the lifelong commitments you have made?
• Commitments can act as both tether and restraint. How do your commitments ground you; how do they restrict you?
• How do you cope with the limits placed on you by the commitments in your life? Which limits do you fight? Do you sometimes hide behind your commitments?

… lives are the poorer for not being at home in the moment, not being able to accept the present circumstances. When stability is not practiced, each moment, each deed, each thought becomes only a step to something else, rather than having inherent work and dignity in itself. (Paul Wilkes, p. 66)

In each moment
• What concrete steps do you take to practice the discipline of mindfulness and attentiveness to God's presence in your daily life?
• What distracts you? How do you cope with distractions? Do you sometimes welcome them?

Yet, all things are to be done with moderation on account of the fainthearted.

A step to something else
• Have you used a situation or a person merely as a stepping stone to something "better"?
• When have you been so focused on the future—arriving at your destination or anticipating an upcoming event—that you failed to appreciate the present moment?

Stewardship

[The cellarer] *will regard all utensils and goods of the monastery as sacred vessels of altar, aware that nothing is to be neglected.* Chapter 31:10-11 (RB 1980: The Rule of St. Benedict in English)

Sacred vessels
• How diligently do you take care of your belongings? Do you regard them as disposable and easily replaced?
• What possessions do you hold tightly? Which do you share readily?
• In what ways are your possessions and self-esteem intertwined? Do some of your possessions make statements about you or reflect your worth as a person?
• Has your determination to cling to an idea or a possession gotten in the way of a relationship?

We have lost a sense of enoughness. (Chittister, The Rule of Benedict, p. 69)

With his good gifts which are in us, we must obey him at all times.

How much is enough?

• When you are contemplating a purchase, do you distinguish between wanting and needing it?

• Are there items in your home—clothes that have not been worn and utensils that are not used—that someone else might find useful? What prevents you from giving them away?

• How easily are you seduced into buying items that you do not need just because they are on sale?

Living a Balanced Life

Yet, all things are to be done with moderation on account of the fainthearted. Chapter 48:9 (RB 1980: The Rule of St. Benedict in English)

Done with moderation

• Chart your various activities. What things do you do to excess?

• What do you neglect or avoid altogether?

• Do your activities reflect your priorities? Are you spending time on what you believe to be important?

On account of the fainthearted

• How willing are you to accommodate others who are less capable, less diligent, less enthusiastic or less ambitious than you are?

Excitable, anxious, extreme, obstinate,
jealous or oversuspicious he must not be.
Such a man is never at rest.

• Are there times when you are the fainthearted member of a group?
• Have there been situations in which your attitude negatively affected another person or a group?

Ora et labora speaks to an appropriate/healthful balance in life. (Casey, p. 52)

Healthy balance
• What are the rhythms of your life? How do you stay grounded when your schedule gets busy or when added demands are placed on you?
• How do you create space for prayer and reflection in a crowded schedule?

Obedience

The labor of obedience will bring you back to God from whom you had drifted through the sloth of disobedience. Prologue 2 (RB 1980: The Rule of St. Benedict in English)

Choosing your actions
• When have you deliberately chosen to turn away from doing what you believed to be good, or just, or true?
• When have you chosen to do what is easiest rather than what is best?
• When have your actions been guided by what is in your best interest rather than by serving the common good?

We must believe that God is always with us.

• Paradoxically, neglecting to make a decision is, in effect, to make a decision. When have you turned away from the good, through indecision, apathy, carelessness or laziness?
• When has concern for doing *exactly the right thing* prevented you from doing anything at all?

Obedience consists of a word spoken and heard: the Latin word behind "obedience" means "listening." (Stewart, p. 54)

Listening
• The world is noisy; our lives are filled with sounds and competing voices. Whose voices shape your thoughts and guide your actions?
• With whom do you consult to help you discern God's voice from other voices?

Hospitality

All guests who present themselves are to be welcomed as Christ, for he himself will say, "I was a stranger and you welcomed me" (Matt. 25:35). Chapter 53:1 (RB 1980: The Rule of St. Benedict in English)

An attitude of welcome
• List instances in the past month when you have extended hospitality to someone. When did you refuse? What were you willing to share and what did you withhold? Why?

See how the Lord in his love shows us the way of life.

• How do you receive people who are new? Do you take the initiative to welcome them or hang back? Do you feel curious or threatened?
• Do you make room in your life for people whose thoughts, opinions or beliefs vary from yours?
• Do you search for the image of God written on the hearts of those you meet, live with and work with?

Hospitality is the willingness to be interrupted and inconvenienced... (Chittister, Wisdom Distilled from the Daily, p. 131)

Responding with grace
• Recall recent instances when you were interrupted or inconvenienced. How did you respond? Were you gracious? Did you grumble? Did you feel resentful?

Prayer

Whenever we want to ask some favor from a powerful man, we do it humbly and respectfully, for fear of presumption. How much more important, then, to lay our petitions before the Lord God of all things with the utmost humility and sincere devotion. We must know that God regards our purity of heart and our tears of compunction, not our many words. Prayer should therefore be short and pure, unless it is prolonged under the inspiration of divine grace. Chapter 20:1-4 (RB 1980: The Rule of St. Benedict in English)

After all, it is written: Never do to another what you do not want done to yourself.

Taking time for prayer
• Do you create space in your life for personal and communal experiences of prayer?
• Do you approach prayer with a list of requests or are you open to the requests God makes of you?
• How does your prayer life shape your actions? How do your actions shape your prayer life?

Prayer is the only way I can live mindfully, ready to encounter the inward grace present all around me, the unfolding "mysticism of everyday life." (Wilkes, p. 174)

Open to grace
• What are the blinders you wear preventing you from seeing God in certain people or circumstances?
• When have you refused the gift of God's grace?
• When have your preconceptions blinded you from recognizing God's work in your life?

Work

Idleness is the enemy of the soul. Therefore, the brothers should have specified periods for manual labor as well as for prayerful reading. Chapter 48:1 (RB 1980: The Rule of St. Benedict in English)

Using your gifts
• What is your life's work?
• How is your work an act of worship?

The eleventh step of humility is that a monk speaks with becoming modesty, briefly and reasonably, but without raising his voice.

• How is your work a means of stewarding and cultivating your gifts and talents?

The purpose of work is to enable me to get more human and to make my world more just. (Chittister, The Rule of Benedict, p. 83)

Making a contribution
• How does your work contribute to the community?
• What steps can you take toward humanizing your workplace: to foster respect, compassion, cooperation among your co-workers?
• How can you facilitate care for the earth at your workplace?

Accountability

Should a brother wish to read privately, let them do so, but without disturbing the others. Chapter 48:5 (RB 1980: The Rule of St. Benedict in English)

Relationships
• When have you placed your own desires ahead of the needs of the communities of family, friends, workplace or neighborhood?
• When have your words or actions undermined trust and respect in your relationships?

If we wish to dwell in the tent of this kingdom, we will never arrive unless we run there by doing good deeds.

Accountability galvanizes community, marking the difference between mere cohabitation and genuinely common purpose. (Stewart, p. 53)

Common purpose
• Are your circles of family and friendship sustained by convenience or by common purpose?
• In what ways do your relationships evoke the best in you and in others?

Do not be daunted immediately by fear and run away from the road that leads to salvation. It is bound to be narrow at the outset. But as we progress in this way of life and faith, we shall run in the paths of God's commandments, our hearts overflowing with the inexpressible delight of love. (Rule of St. Benedict, Prologue 48-49)

Listen readily to holy reading.

Bibliography

Casey, Michael. *A Guide to Living in the Truth: Saint Benedict's Teaching on Humility*. Liguori, Missouri: Ligouri/Triumph, 1999, 2001.

Chittister, Joan. *The Rule of Benedict: Insight for the Ages*. New York: Crossroad, 1993.

_____, *Wisdom Distilled from the Daily: Living the Rule of St. Benedict Today*. San Francisco: Harper, 1990.

Ford, Hugh. "St. Benedict of Nursia." *The Catholic Encyclopedia*. Vol. 2. New York: Robert Appleton Company, 1907. 17 Mar. 2009 <http://www.newadvent.org/cathen/02467b.htm>.

Fry, Timothy, ed. *RB 80: The Rule of St. Benedict in English*. Collegeville: The Liturgical Press, 1982.

Stewart, Columba. *Prayer and Community: The Benedictine Tradition*. New York: Orbis Books, 1998.

Vest, Norveen. Cited in *Oblate Formation Booklet*. St. Vincent Archabbey, Latrobe, PA. Revised 2002.

Wilkes, Paul. *Beyond the Walls: Monastic Wisdom for Everyday Life*. New York: Image Books, 1999.

Trusting in God's help, he must
in love obey.

The Ten Commandments

1. I am the Lord, thy God, thou shalt not have any gods before me.

2. Thou shalt not take the name of the Lord, thy God, in vain.

3. Remember to keep holy the Sabbath Day.

4. Honor thy father and thy mother.

5. Thou shalt not kill.

6. Thou shalt not commit adultery.

7. Thou shalt not steal.

8. Thou shalt not bear false witness against thy neighbor.

9. Thou shalt not covet thy neighbor's wife.

10. Thou shalt not covet thy neighbor's goods.

Whoever needs less should thank God and not be distressed.

Like the deer that yearns
For running streams

So my soul is yearning
For you, my God. PSALM 41

The Corporal Works of Mercy

To feed the hungry.
To give drink to the thirsty.
To clothe the naked.
To visit and ransom captives.
To give shelter to the homeless.
To visit the sick.
To bury the dead.

The Spiritual Works of Mercy

To admonish sinners.
To instruct the ignorant.
To counsel the doubtful.
To comfort the sorrowful.
To bear wrongs patiently.
To forgive all injuries.
To pray for the living and the dead.

---

*They should each try to be the first to show
respect to the other.*

Act of Contrition

O my God,
I am heartily sorry for having offended thee,
and I detest all my sins
because of thy just punishments,
but most of all because they offend thee my God,
who art all good and deserving of all my love.
I firmly resolve, with the help of thy grace,
to sin no more,
and to avoid the near occasions of sin.

Amen.

SUGGESTED PSALMS: 51 and 32
(see pages 65 and 81)

Speak the truth with heart and tongue.

Just for Today—A Plan for Living

Live one day at a time; handle my personal challenges for today only. Yesterday's gone; tomorrow may not come. Today is mine.

Just for Today, I will try to live through this day only and not tackle my whole life's problems at once. I can do something for twelve hours that would appall me if I felt that I had to keep it up for a lifetime.

Just for Today, I will be happy. This assumes to be true what Abraham Lincoln said, that, "Most folks are as happy as they make their minds up to be."

Just for Today, I will adjust myself to what is, and not try to adjust everything to my own desires. I will take my luck as it comes, and fit myself to it.

Just for Today, I will try to strengthen my mind. I will study. I will learn something useful. I will not be a mental loafer. I will read something that requires effort, thought and concentration.

Just for Today, I will exercise my soul in three ways: I will do somebody a good turn and not get found out. If anyone knows of it, it will not count. I will do at least two things I don't want to do—just for exercise. And I will not show anyone that my feelings are hurt. They may be hurt, but today I will not show it.

Speaking and teaching are the master's task; the disciple is to be silent and listen.

Just for Today, I will have a program. I may not follow it exactly, but I will have it. I will save myself from two pests: hurry and indecision.

Just for Today, I will have a quiet half hour all by myself and relax. During this half hour, I will try to get a better perspective of my life.

Just for Today, I will be unafraid. Especially, I will not be afraid to enjoy what is beautiful and to believe that as I give to the world, so the world will give to me.

Just for Today, I will be agreeable. I will look as good as I can, dress becomingly, talk low, act courteously, criticize not one bit, not find fault with anything and try not to improve or regulate anybody except myself.

The twelfth step of humility is that a monk always manifests humility in his bearing no less than in his heart.

De Profundis

De profundis clamavi ad te, Domine;
Domine exaudi vocem meam.
Fiant aures tuae intendentes
in vocem deprecationis meae.

Si iniquitates observaveris, Domine,
Domine, quis sustinebit?
Quia apud te propitiatio est,
et timebimus te.
Sustinui te, Domine,
sustinuit anima mea in verbo eius,
speravit anima mea in Domino.

Magis quam custodes auroram
speret Israel in Domino.
Quia apud Dominum misericordia,
et copiosa apud eum redemptio.
Et ipse redimet Israel
ex omnibus iniquitatibus eius.

Place your hope in God alone.

(128) 129. A Prayer of Repentance and Trust: Sixth Psalm of Repentance

1.   Out of the depths I cry to you, O Lord,
2   Lord, hear my voice!
     O let your ears be attentive
     to the voice of my pleading.

3   If you, O Lord, should mark our guilt,
     Lord, who would survive?
4   But with you is found forgiveness:
     for this we revere you.

5   My soul is waiting for the Lord.
     I count on God's word.
6   My soul is longing for the Lord
     more than those who watch for daybreak
     (Let the watchers count on daybreak
7   and Israel on the Lord.)

     Because with the Lord there is mercy
     and fullness of redemption,
8   Israel indeed God will redeem
     from all its iniquity.

---

*What is not possible to us by nature,
let us ask the Lord to supply by the help
of his grace.*

THEMATIC INDEX

	149	93
	150	94
Marriage Blessing	(126) 127	87
	(129) 128	64
Morning Prayer	5	27
	8	74
	(117) 118	22
Night Prayers	4	80
	(15) 16	32
	(90) 91	33
	(133) 134	55
	(129) 130	64
In Old Age	(70) 71	41
	(89) 90	62
Terminal Illness	(38) 39	50
In Thanksgiving	(66) 67	44
In Time of Need	6	29
Trust in God	(15) 16	32
	(22) 23	61
	(24) 25	57
	(26) 27	45
	(45) 46	67

GENERAL INDEX